A Guide to Staff Employment in General Practice

Royal College of
General Practitioners

A Guide to Staff Employment in General Practice

Jim Milligan

The Royal College of General Practitioners was founded in 1952 with this object:

'To encourage, foster and maintain the highest possible standards in general practice and for that purpose to take or join with others in taking steps consistent with the charitable nature of that object which may assist towards the same.'

Among its responsibilities under its Royal Charter the College is entitled to:

'Diffuse information on all matters affecting general practice and issue such publications as may assist the object of the College.'

British Library Cataloguing-in-Publication Data
A catalogue record for this book is available from the British Library

© Royal College of General Practitioners, 2015
Published by the Royal College of General Practitioners, 2015
30 Euston Square, London NW1 2FB

All rights reserved. No part of this publication may be reproduced, stored in a retrieval system or transmitted, in any form or by any means, electronic, mechanical, photocopying, recording or otherwise without the prior permission of the Royal College of General Practitioners.

Printed by Lightning Source UK Ltd
Indexed by Susan Leech

ISBN 978-0-85084-386-6

Contents

Preface viii
Acknowledgements ix

1. **Preliminaries** 1
   Legalities 1
   Formation of contract 2
   Workers' rights 3
   Rights not requiring a contract as such 3
   Agency staff 4
   A cautionary tale 5

2. **The contract of employment** 7
   The law 7
   What is in the contract? 7
   Changing the contract 9
   Dismissal 10
   Breach of contract 10
   Employment scenarios 12

3. **Managing disciplinary procedures** 13
   Disciplinary procedures 13
   Appeals 16
   How to conduct a formal disciplinary meeting 16
   Employment scenarios 19

4. **Performance management** 21
   Behaviour 21

Disability 24
Capability 26
Misconduct 27
Managing sickness absence 27
Bullying and harassment 32
Employment scenarios 35

5. Terminating the contract 37
Ending the contract 37
Notice periods and pay 37
Dismissal 38
Handling dismissal in the workplace 40
Constructive dismissal 42
Redundancy 43
Employment scenarios 45

6. Specific legal issues 47
Statutory rights 47
Maternity rights 48
Paternity leave and pay 51
Equality rights 55
Statutory leave entitlement 56
Parental leave 58
Flexible working 59
Part-time employees 63
Temporary contracts 64
Health and safety 67
Employment scenarios 68

7. Other issues 71
Staff appraisal 71
Workplace stress 75
Example of a stress policy 78
Grievance procedures 80
Transfer of Undertakings – TUPE 82

8. **Recent developments** 85
   GP federations 85
   Employment tribunal changes 86
   New health and work service in England and Wales 87

Appendix I: Useful sources of information 89
Appendix II: Statutory payments 91
Appendix III: Written statement of employment particulars 95
Appendix IV: Guidance on disciplinary procedures 97
Appendix V: Employment tribunals 101
Appendix VI: The Equality Act 2010 105
Appendix VII: Absence records template 113
Appendix VIII: Self-appraisal form 115
Appendix IX: Workplace discussions 117
Appendix X: Employment scenarios – with comments 119
Index 127

Preface

This is a practical guide for GPs and practice managers to help them navigate the ever-changing backdrop of employment law. It is based on my experience of advising, representing and training practices. Regular updates will be available.

Written contracts are essential, but more is needed if employees are to be managed reasonably. Due consideration should be given to the legal issues involved before any (formal) action is taken by an employer. Such consideration should be accompanied by clear, fair and consistent management if running an efficient practice is to be achieved.

I believe that this guide will assist staff partners and practice managers in developing their understanding of and procedures in staff management. This guide is intended for the non-lawyer who has to grapple on a regular basis with the quirks of both human psychology and the law. Most chapters end with some relevant practical problems for the reader to consider. Suggested responses are given in an appendix.

The content is for general information purposes and is not intended to constitute legal or specific professional advice. Legal information is provided for guidance only and should not be regarded as an authoritative statement of the law, which can only be made by reference to the particular circumstances that apply. If problems arise it is therefore always wise to seek legal advice at the time.

Jim Milligan
Practice Adviser
www.jim-milligan.co.uk

Acknowledgements

In compiling this guide I have drawn on material from the following:

- Acas[1] (very good for practical advice on procedural matters)
- Gov.uk website[2] (very good for specific employment rights)
- the Health and Safety Executive[3]
- the Department of Justice – Courts and Tribunals Judiciary (home of Employment Appeal Tribunal written judgments).[4]

The information and material on these websites is subject to Crown copyright protection and is used under the terms of the Open Government Licence for public sector information.[5]

I am also grateful to the Chartered Institute of Personnel and Development (CIPD)[6] for allowing me to quote from their *Absence Management 2014* survey report.

References

1. Acas. www.acas.org.uk.
2. Working, jobs and pensions. www.gov.uk/browse/working [accessed 13 November 2014].
3. Health and Safety Executive. www.hse.gov.uk.
4. Courts and Tribunals Judiciary. www.employmentappeals.gov.uk/public/recentjudgments.aspx [accessed 6 January 2015]
5. Open Government Licence. www.nationalarchives.gov.uk/doc/open-government-licence/version/3/ [accessed 13 November 2014].
6. CIPD. www.cipd.co.uk.

1

Preliminaries

Legalities
Formation of contract
Workers' rights
Rights not requiring a contract as such
Agency staff
A cautionary tale

First a note about devolution. Employment law is not a devolved matter in any part of the UK. However, there are three differing legal systems – England and Wales, Northern Ireland and Scotland. This means that they may have different institutions and different procedures, but essentially the same employment law.

Legalities

Now, this section concerns the legal aspects of an *employment* contract – but, before you read on, here is the point. The aim is not to turn practice managers into lawyers (or partners into judges); it is to keep you out of the clutches of employment tribunals (and lawyers).

Although staff management in a practice is absolutely *not* a legal forum, it can often help to consider the legal elements of any issue before proceeding. This may keep you out of a very legal forum called an employment tribunal. In my experience it is relatively rare for a practice to be drawn into a tribunal, but when it does it can be a traumatic experience – being judged in a forum that is part of the UK legal system. It can also be very expensive. The highest ever compensation in a UK employment tribunal, a discrimination case in 2011, cost an employer £4.5m.

Coming back to the practice setting, a partner or practice manager is *not* required to act as a lawyer would. However, to avoid the many pitfalls in staff management, knowledge of the relevant law in any given situation can be a life-saver. Fortunately you will generally have time to back off and check matters, which is not a bad thing anyway.

The way to approach this is that, like it or not, an employment contract is a legal entity creating legal obligations on both employer and employee. In the first instance you may need to establish whether or not a (legal) contract exists, and, if so, what is in it. Remember that, under the law, for a contract to be enforceable it does not have to be in writing (unless you are buying a house).

Formation of contract

So, how to establish whether a legal contract exists and what that implies? Offer and acceptance are two of the elements required for the formation of a legally binding contract.

An offer to contract on certain terms by an employer to a prospective employee and an indication by the latter of its acceptance of those terms indicates that a contract has been formed. The other elements traditionally required for a legally binding contract are consideration (payment) and an intention to create legal relations.

All of the four conditions above are satisfied in the employment context, so we have a contract that is legally binding on both parties. This contract is the key to employment rights, since 'employees' have 'employment' rights.

Issue of written contracts

There is no requirement to issue a written contract to an employee. However, a contract of employment exists in law as soon as an employee starts work and it is advisable to put this in writing. Starting work demonstrates that the employee accepts the terms and conditions offered by the employer, and both employer and employee are bound by these terms.

A contract may be verbally agreed and not written down. Most employees are however entitled by law to be given a written statement setting out the main particulars of their employment. This statement will not necessarily cover every aspect of the contract, but will provide important evidence of the main terms and conditions.

Written statement of employment particulars

This 'written statement' must be given to an employee if his or her employment lasts at least a month. This is not an employment contract as such but it will include the main conditions of employment. See Appendix III for a complete list of the items required to be stated. Alternatively employers can download a template of a written statement of particulars to fill in.[1]

The employer must provide the written statement within two months of the start of employment.

An alternative to issuing the written particulars is to issue an unsigned contract – perhaps labelled as a draft – to show what the terms of the contract are. So long as this draft contract is comprehensive it will satisfy the legal requirement to issue written particulars of the terms of employment.

In Northern Ireland, a written statement must explain what the disciplinary rules and procedures are.[2]

In addition there are a number of employment-related rights enjoyed, in the European context, by 'workers' who may not have *any* form of contractual relationship with an employer. So let us look at who has 'employment' rights without an employment contract.

Workers' rights

Some individuals will have certain rights even though they are not an employee so long as they are a 'worker' under the law. A worker is defined in the Employment Rights Act as someone who is an employee *or* who personally performs work in return for payment. The latter could include a GP locum, or someone else doing work for the practice in a self-employed capacity.

A *worker* is entitled, among other things, to a statutory minimum 28 days of holiday and enrolment in a pension plan (if one exists), not to mention the right to equal treatment under the equality laws (see Appendix VI).

Rights not requiring a contract as such

It is unlawful to discriminate against anyone under the Equality Act (see Appendix VI). This includes job applicants who are not yet under contract to the practice (see the section on appointing staff, overleaf).

Employee rights

In addition to rights written down in an employment contract there are many other legal rights. These are enshrined in statutes or in decisions handed down in the appellate courts through case law. Legally there is a divide between self-employed people, who are free to contract for any terms they wish, and *employees*, who are covered by the many and various employment laws.

Under the Employment Rights Act an 'employee' means an individual who has entered into or works under a contract of employment, and 'contract of employment' means a contract of service or apprenticeship, whether express or implied, and (if it is express) whether oral or in writing.

Appointing staff

Remember, job applicants are covered by equality legislation. So, to state the obvious, employers must not announce or imply in a job advert that they will discriminate against anyone. This includes saying that the work does not cater for workers with a disability or a young person is sought. For more information about disability rights, see Chapter 4.

Only use phrases like 'recent graduate' or 'highly experienced' when these are actual *requirements* of the job. This could discriminate against younger or older people who might not have had the opportunity to obtain certain qualifications.

Where an employer advertises could be indirect discrimination – for example, advertising only in men's magazines.

When you can discriminate

An employer can only specify that the successful applicant will be from a particular group if it is a requirement of the job. For example, people under 18 cannot legally sell alcohol.

Agency staff

The Agency Workers Regulations 2010 were established to combat discrimination of people who work for employment agencies. They state that agency workers should be no less favourably treated in pay and working time than their permanent counterparts who do the same work.

The regulations cover agency workers supplied by a temporary work agency to a hirer. This includes most agency workers that people refer to as 'temps'. The regulations also cover agency workers supplied via intermediaries.

The regulations do not cover the genuinely self-employed, individuals working through their own limited liability company, or individuals working on managed service contracts.

The regulations give agency workers the entitlement to the same or no less favourable treatment as comparable employees with respect to basic employment and working conditions, if and when they complete a qualifying period of 12 weeks in a particular job.

Agency workers are classed as 'workers' rather than as employees. All workers, including agency workers, are entitled to certain rights that include:

- paid annual leave

- rest breaks and limits on working time
- the National Minimum Wage
- no unlawful deductions from wages
- discrimination rights under the Equality Act 2010 (see Appendix VI)
- health and safety at work (see Chapter 6).

A cautionary tale

As an illustration of how contracts can be constructed in a legal forum let me offer this.

A few years ago when I was living in the Scottish Borders I worked as a volunteer at the Citizens Advice Bureau (CAB) in Hawick. One day a client came in saying she had been sacked without notice and asked what her rights were.

The client had worked from home for a charity based in Glasgow. Her job was to telephone people from a list given to her each week to seek donations. She was told the hours she could call people and she had no holiday entitlement.

I asked if she had a written contract. She produced the documentation she had been given by the charity. It consisted of three or four pages and across the top of the first page were the words 'this is not a contract'.

This 'contract not' document included hours of duty, pay and the statement that no tax was being deducted; the job holder was responsible for this. The document was signed on behalf of the charity *and by my client*. Just above the space for the signatures were those words again, 'this is not a contract'.

Where to go? My client had signed a document showing that she agreed it was 'not a contract'.

As it happens there is no one single test to determine whether a worker is employed or self-employed. Tribunals and courts have developed a number of tests that combine a range of factors to decide whether a worker is an employee or self-employed.

These tests look at the reality of – not the label on – the *relationship* between the worker and the organisation for which he or she is carrying out work.

Assisted by the CAB's Scottish legal department we brought a preliminary hearing in the employment tribunal in Edinburgh to decide the status of my client. Was she an employee who was entitled to employment rights involving unfair dismissal and redundancy? Or was she a 'worker' with none of these rights?

Happily (for my client) the tribunal ruled that, notwithstanding 'this is not a contract', she was in reality an employee within the meaning of the act.

We proceeded to a full hearing and my client received compensation for unfair dismissal, redundancy, outstanding holiday pay and failure to give the required statutory notice of termination.

For me, the legal lesson here is you cannot rely on the words alone when determining employment status. As a wise old judge once said, 'If it walks like a duck and it quacks ... it's a duck!'

The status tests are shown on Table 1.1.

Table 1.1: Relevant factors in the assessment of employment status

Mutuality of obligation. Does the employer have to provide work and does the worker have to do the work?	Whether the worker works only for the organisation concerned
The purpose and intention of the parties. What was in the minds of the parties when the contract was formed?	Whether the worker is integrated into the organisation
How much control does the worker have over the work – where, when and how?	Element of financial risk on the part of the worker
Method of pay – salary/wages or invoiced fees?	Fixed hours and regular work. If the worker works fixed hours doing the same kind of work all the time, it is likely that he or she is an employee. If he or she is free to decide the type of work taken on and how and when he or she does it, the worker is more likely to be self-employed
No or only minor provision of tools and equipment	
Work performed at employer's premises	
Whether the worker has to give a personal service. A worker who may suggest a colleague to cover for him or her is likely to be self-employed	Presence of sick pay scheme and a disciplinary procedure. The presence of either of these would indicate an employment contract

References

1. Employment particulars written statement: form. www.gov.uk/government/publications/employment-particulars-written-statement-form [accessed 13 November 2014].
2. NIdirect. Written statement of employment particulars. www.nidirect.gov.uk/written-statement-of-employment-particulars [accessed 13 November 2014].

2

The contract of employment

The law
What is in the contract?
Changing the contract
Dismissal
Breach of contract
Employment scenarios

The law

As we saw in the previous chapter, the contract of employment is a legally binding *agreement* (not necessarily in writing) between employer and employee. It is formed when the employee agrees to an offer of work and the employer agrees to pay wages for the work.

Note that there is no legal requirement that the 'agreement' be put in writing (although this is recommended). However, it is a legal requirement for employers to give employees a *written statement* of the employment particulars (see Appendix III). If a model contract is followed, this will generally incorporate the written particulars required, so a separate statement is unnecessary.

What is in the contract?

It is well-established law that in any contract there are not only *express* (written) terms but also *implied* (unwritten) terms. The latter includes terms such as the requirement to obey reasonable and lawful instructions.

Over time the courts have developed guidelines to the circumstances in which they may be prepared to imply other terms into a contract of employment. Basically, the term must be one that is so common that it must be taken to have been implicitly agreed.

The contract therefore will include:

- *express terms*, which are terms set down *in writing*
- *implied terms*, which may include those that are too obvious to mention (e.g. that the employee will not steal from the employer) or those that are the custom and practice of the 'industry'
- *terms incorporated* into individual contracts by reference to other documents, such as practice handbooks
- *terms imposed by law* (e.g. the right not to be discriminated against on the grounds of age, sex, race, disability, etc.).

Implied terms – duties of employees

There are numerous terms that only come into their own when, in a court of law, it becomes necessary to define them. They exist in most contracts nevertheless. One example is the duty of an employee to take reasonable care of the employer's property, normally implied if not expressly set out in the employee's contract. Duties of an employee that are frequently implied rather than set out as express terms include:

- to cooperate with the employer
- to obey reasonable and lawful instructions
- to exercise reasonable care and skill, to be reasonably competent
- to take reasonable care of the employer's property
- a duty of confidentiality, which if it concerns patients can continue after the employment has ended
- to act in good faith and fidelity
- to adapt to reasonable changes
- to maintain a relationship of trust and confidence.

A breach of any of the above duties by an employee may lead to the employer taking disciplinary action. In exceptional circumstances an employer may claim damages from the employee where a financial loss has occurred. However, employers must be careful not to take the law into their own hands by making unauthorised deductions from wages, say, so it is prudent to seek expert advice in any but the simplest case.

Implied terms – employers

Implied terms also apply to the employer's responsibilities. A selection of the terms that an employer may be legally obliged to comply with is:

- to pay wages
- to provide support
- not to treat employees in an arbitrary or vindictive manner
- to provide a safe system of work
- to inform employees of important decisions
- to take reasonable care
- to allow access to grievance procedures
- to maintain trust and confidence
- to give support against harassment
- not to undermine a supervisor's authority.

Changing the contract

Contracts of employment in practice change throughout their existence. Most changes take place by mutual agreement. For example, employees will not normally object to pay rises or promotions. Problems arise, however, when one party – normally the employer – wants to change the contract and the other party does not agree to it.

Legally, a contract can only be changed by mutual consent. Unilaterally imposed changes will *not* be contractually binding unless the other party agrees to them. The terms of an individual employment contract however can be changed in various ways, as follows:

- employer and employee may agree on the change
- the contract itself may provide, either expressly or by implication, for changes
- individual contracts may be varied by a collective agreement that will be binding on individual employees (not generally applicable in general practice)
- the employee may accept a change by conduct, e.g. by working under the changed contract without protest.

The employer may simply implement the changes in the contract. This constitutes a unilateral variation by the employer. The latter two situations are covered below.

Acceptance by conduct

An employee's agreement to a variation in contract (like the contract itself) does not have to be formal or in writing, although it is to be recommended. Failure to give a written statement notifying a change will not in itself render the change ineffective, but the absence of such may subsequently be treated as indicative that there was no such variation.

Employers may (and often do) impose unilateral changes without consent. If an employee simply carries on under the revised terms, he or she will eventually be taken to have acquiesced in them. However, this approach is not advised because of the negative effects on staff morale generally.

Unilateral variation

In the absence of agreement, an employer may decide that the reasons for the variation are so compelling that he or she will press ahead regardless and implement it without the employee's agreement. There are two ways in which this can be done:

- the change is announced as a *fait accompli*, or
- a new contract may be offered in place of the existing one.

A unilateral change amounts to a *breach of contract* by the employer. An employee can respond in one of four ways:

- acquiescence in the change
- resignation, followed by a claim for constructive dismissal (see Chapter 5)
- refusal to work under the new terms
- bring an action for breach of contract in an employment tribunal or small claims court (the Sheriff Court in Scotland) while still employed.

Dismissal

In an employment tribunal, *business necessity* may justify a change in contractual terms that leads to *dismissal*. The Court of Appeal in England has held that a *sound, good business reason* would constitute Some Other Substantial Reason for dismissing an employee who refuses to go along with organisational changes requiring changes in an individual contract. Nevertheless a 'sound business' reason would have to involve a potentially large loss of income.

Breach of contract

However, if an employee brings an action for *breach of contract*, all he or she has to do is to show that there has been a breach. It is *no defence* for the employer to say that there were sound business reasons for his or her actions, or that the employer acted reasonably in the circumstances. Such arguments may be persuasive before tribunals in unfair dismissal cases, but will cut no ice when the claim is for breach of contract in a civil court.

Not all breaches of contract by employers are amenable to actions for damages however. Such damages can only arise where there is direct financial loss arising from the breach.

The employer's final method for changing the contract is to terminate with proper notice and offer a new contract on the revised terms. There will be no breach of contract if this is done, but the termination of the old contract (i.e. dismissal) could give rise to an unfair dismissal claim. A tribunal will then have to assess the employer's *reasonableness*. Tribunals have accepted that an employer's 'urgent' need to reduce expenditure, for example, could justify contractual changes. As ever, legal advice should be sought if this step is contemplated.

Summary

If an employee refuses to agree to a change that would vary his or her contract, two options are left to the employer. One is that it may be felt that the change is not necessary, so it is not implemented. The other is that, if the change is reasonable and it results from the needs of the business, it may be enforced, so long as it can be justified. However, this will require prior consultation with employees. Only then should unilateral changes be imposed.

A practice faced with opposition to proposed changes is urged to take advice from the British Medical Association on the matter at the earliest possible stage.

Ending the contract

If the employer terminates the contract this is generally dismissal and the appropriate procedures must be followed (see Chapter 5 for dismissal).

If the employee terminates the contract this is generally resignation with appropriate notice, details of which should be set out in the contract. Alternatively the employee may apparently resign but it may be held to be a form of dismissal – constructive dismissal (see Chapter 5).

How to get it right

- Issue employees with a *written contract* – signed by both parties – setting out the main terms and conditions of their employment within two months of them starting work. Ideally this should be done as soon as possible, e.g. when the employee starts.

- Consult with staff first before making any changes that affect contracts.
- Verbally agree any subsequent change with employees and then put it in writing – signed by both parties.
- Remember, if you terminate a contract you should follow the advisory dismissal procedure as well as giving at least the statutory minimum notice period (or the notice period agreed in the contract if this is longer). NB: Advice should be taken before this is done.
- Put as much as possible in writing to avoid misunderstandings. If unsure, seek advice.

Employment scenarios

1. The practice has been invited to bid for the provision of a surgery at a local supermarket. Staff contracts show the location and hours that are worked at present.

   Could employees be made to staff the supermarket surgery?

2. It transpires that your most recently appointed receptionist has, by an oversight, not been issued with a written contract. She now wants to change her shifts and says that, anyway, nothing has been agreed about the hours she works.

   What is the position?

3

Managing disciplinary procedures

Disciplinary procedures
Appeals
How to conduct a formal disciplinary meeting
Employment scenarios

Disciplinary procedures

Rules

Rules set standards of conduct at work. They should be fair, reflect the needs of the practice and be written in a way that everyone understands.

If staff know and accept the rules, they will be less likely to break them. Rules help ensure a consistency of management action and can improve efficiency.

Practice rules may cover:

- timekeeping
- absence
- holidays
- health and safety
- standards of work
- personal appearance
- use of practice facilities
- smoking
- non-discrimination
- gross misconduct.

Remember: there should not be too many written rules. Be realistic. Consult with employees, and be careful to avoid rules that are unjustifiable and may be unlawful.

Procedure

While the rules set out standards, the disciplinary procedure helps employers deal fairly with employees who fail to maintain those standards. The aim here should be to ensure that the appropriate standards are maintained, not that employees are punished.

Box 3.1: Fair disciplinary procedures

- Establish the facts of each case.
- Inform the employee of the problem.
- Hold a meeting – discuss the problem.
- Allow the employee to be accompanied at the meeting.
- Decide on appropriate action.
- Provide employees with an opportunity to appeal any decision made.

Most disciplinary problems can be solved by informal discussions or counselling. However, if this fails to resolve the problem you will need a more formal approach.

A disciplinary procedure will:

- encourage employees to achieve and maintain standards of behaviour
- provide a fair and consistent method of dealing with alleged failures
- remind managers and supervisors how disciplinary matters should be handled
- minimise disagreements about disciplinary matters
- reduce the need for dismissals.

See Appendix IV for Acas guidance.

The disciplinary procedure should take account of the following principles:

- employers and employees should raise and deal with issues promptly and should not unreasonably delay meetings, decisions or confirmation of those decisions
- employers and employees should act consistently
- employers should carry out all necessary investigations, to establish the

facts of any situation

- employers should inform employees of the perceived details of any problem arising and give them an opportunity to put their case in response before any decisions are made
- employers should allow employees to be accompanied at any formal disciplinary or grievance meeting
- employers should allow an employee to appeal against any formal decision made.

Operating the disciplinary procedure

- Establish the facts before taking action.
- Deal with cases of minor misconduct or unsatisfactory performance informally.
- For more serious cases, follow formal procedures, including informing the employee of the alleged misconduct or unsatisfactory performance.
- Invite the employee to a meeting and inform him or her of the right to be accompanied.
- Where performance is unsatisfactory explain to the employee the improvement required, the support that will be given, and when and how performance will be reviewed.
- If giving a warning, tell the employee why and how he or she needs to change, the consequences of failing to improve, and that he or she has a right to appeal.
- If dismissing an employee, tell them why, when their contract will end and that they can appeal.
- When taking disciplinary action always follow the Acas Code of Practice 2009 (see Appendix IV).
- When dealing with absences from work, determine the reasons for the absence before deciding on what action to take.

Dismissal

Practices should bear in mind that before they dismiss an employee or impose a serious sanction such as a written warning, they must as a minimum have followed the Acas Code (see Appendix IV). A tribunal would take this into account in addition to the *reason* for the dismissal (see Chapter 5).

Appeals

- If the employee wishes to appeal, set up a meeting and inform the employee of his or her right to be accompanied.
- Where possible, arrange for the appeal to be dealt with by a more senior individual not involved with the earlier decision.
- Better still establish an *advisory* panel drawn from outside the practice, the trust's HR person, the practice accountant, Local Medical Committee, etc.
- Inform the employee about the appeal decision and the reasons for it.

Records

Keep written records for future reference, you never know when an employment tribunal is going to arise.

How to conduct a formal disciplinary meeting

Note: not all the steps may be required, particularly if no witnesses are involved.

Preparation

- Gather all the relevant facts such as the employee's personal details and disciplinary record, statements from witnesses and other relevant documents.
- Where possible, check witness statements and evidence for their accuracy.
- Inform the employee of the complaint, the procedure to be followed and his or her rights. Inform the employee which documents they can have access to in advance.
- Consider possible explanations from an employee and, if possible, check them.
- Inform the employee of his or her right to be accompanied to the meeting.
- Allow the employee time to prepare his or her case.
- Arrange a time and place for the meeting, which should be held in as private a location as is possible.
- Allow witnesses to attend, if it is possible to do so, unless the employee accepts their statements as fact.

- Consider the structure of the meeting and the main points that need to be made.
- Arrange to have somebody present to take notes of the proceedings.

At the start
- Introduce all those present and explain why they are there.
- Explain that the purpose of the meeting is to consider whether disciplinary action should be taken, in accordance with your practice's disciplinary procedure.
- Explain how the meeting will be conducted.

Presenting the statement of complaint
- State precisely what the complaint is and outline the case briefly by going through the evidence.
- Make sure the employee, representative or accompanying person is allowed to see any witness statements. Take care with statements given in confidence.
- Establish whether the employee is prepared to accept that he or she may have done something wrong. Then agree the steps to remedy the situation.

During the employee's reply
- Allow them to: state their case and answer any allegations; ask questions; present evidence; and call witnesses.
- Allow them to confer with their representative – who may also ask questions.
- Listen carefully in silence as this may make the employee more forthcoming.
- If a grievance that relates to the case is raised during the meeting it may be appropriate to suspend the meeting for a short while until the grievance can be considered.

There should be a general question and discussion session in order to establish and clarify the case.

- Use this stage to establish all the facts.
- Adjourn the meeting if further investigation appears necessary or if the employee requests it.

- Ask the employee for any explanation for his or her misconduct, or failure to improve, including any special circumstances.
- Stop the proceedings if it becomes clear that the employee has provided an adequate explanation or that there is no real evidence to support the allegation.
- Keep the meeting formal but polite and encourage the employee to speak freely.
- Use questions to clarify any issues and to check what is being said.
- Ask open-ended questions such as 'What happened then?' to get a broad picture.
- Ask closed questions such as those needing a yes/no answer in order to get at specific information.
- Do not get involved in arguments or make personal or humiliating remarks.
- Avoid any physical contact or gestures that could be misinterpreted.

Concluding

- Summarise the main points after questioning is complete. This allows all those present to be reminded of the nature of the offence and the evidence submitted. It also helps to ensure nothing has been missed.
- Ask the employee whether they have anything else to say.

Adjournment

- It is good practice to adjourn the meeting before a decision is taken on what disciplinary action should be taken.
- Adjourning allows time for proper consideration and reflection, and can also be used to check any facts that may have been raised and that could be in dispute.

Problems

- If new facts emerge then consider reconvening the meeting.
- If an employee becomes upset or distressed, allow the employee time to regain his or her composure.
- If an employee is too distressed to continue, adjourn and reconvene at a later date.

- Allowing people to 'let off steam' can be a helpful way of finding out what happened.
- Abusive language or behaviour during the meeting should not be tolerated.

Dismissal

The final step should only be taken if there is no employee improvement to a required level.

Time limits

Apart from special circumstances there should be agreed time limits, after which disciplinary action can be disregarded because of acceptable behaviour or conduct.

- The time limits should be established when the disciplinary procedure is being drawn up.
- You may have different periods for different types of warning.
- Written warnings normally remain on file for up to six months or, in the case of a final written warning, 12–18 months.
- Warnings are generally disregarded, after the specified period, for future disciplinary purposes.
- You can still issue a further warning before a current one expires.

Performance issues

Most will involve either conduct and/or capability. In both cases behaviour may be involved and the disciplinary procedures can be used to modify behaviour (see Chapter 4).

Employment scenarios

1. A patient has complained that a receptionist told her that her daughter was pregnant. She had been unaware of the fact.

    How do you deal with this?

2. A young receptionist appears for work with a stud through her nose.

    Can you do anything about this?

4

Performance management

Behaviour
Disability
Capability
Misconduct
Managing sickness absence
Bullying and harassment
Employment scenarios

The aim of performance management is to continuously maintain and, where possible, improve the performance of individuals and that of the practice. It involves making sure that the performance of employees contributes to the goals of their teams and the practice as a whole.

Behaviour

This whole topic is essentially about change, change in staff behaviour. The 'behaviour' may be focused on the job being done, or the interpersonal relationships – with patients and colleagues – inherent in the job being done. In both cases the focus is on *job issues*, not the person as such. However, the *behaviour* of the job holder necessarily may become the focus.

It is several years now since 'retirement age' could be used as a reason for terminating the contracts of older employees. One outcome of this has been an increased emphasis on performance management as a way of ensuring that (all) employees' performance is appropriate to their job.

It is recognised that this has to be managed either by discussion or by formal performance management procedures. For all employees an employer should ensure that any poor performance is addressed with them. This requires fair, objective procedures to be in place for managing performance.

In the first instance this may lead to 'management by exception', i.e. only dealing with performance that is outside the norm, or not adequate. This requires appraisal (in the general sense) and analysis of why someone is not performing to the required standard. Only then can a strategy be put in place. Triggers might include complaints from patients or colleagues, attendance problems or mistakes on the job.

Although Figure 4.1 ends with 'improvement or dismissal', the aim is not simply to get to the dismissal stage – it is to encourage improvement.

Figure 4.1: **Dealing with poor performance**

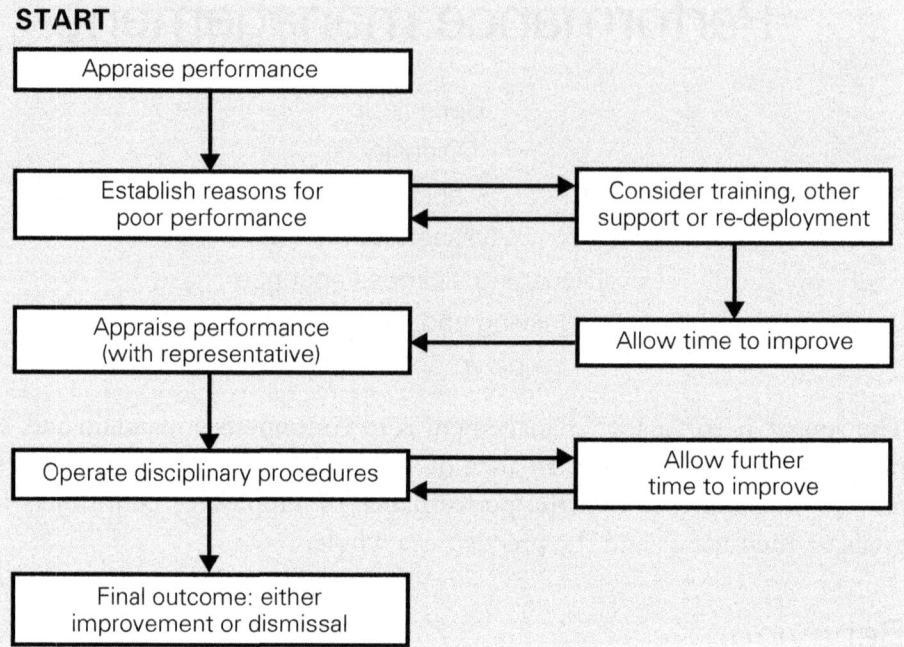

Workplace discussions

Regardless of the age of employees, Acas advises discussing with them their future aims and aspirations. This can help identify their training or development needs and provides an opportunity for the employer to discuss future work requirements and how these impact on the employee.

These elements may be new for some practices whereas for others it may be a normal part of their appraisal process. It is for the practice to decide whether or not to hold workplace discussions but they can be a good way of raising issues before they become acute problems, including the performance of older employees.

Whatever the size of the practice, these discussions should be simple, informal and confidential. Set out below is an agenda for managing these discussions:

Areas to talk about

- Future plans (from employer).
- Aims and aspirations (from employee).
- Performance to date against targets, activities and outcomes.
- Developmental or training needs.
- Future performance.

Such discussions are best undertaken voluntarily and in an atmosphere of trust, allowing for the fact that the employer does need to be able to plan workforce requirements to meet future business needs.

Employees have a right to be treated fairly and should participate in these discussions in as open and frank a manner as they possibly can. The discussions do not have to follow exactly the same agenda for all employees irrespective of where they are in their careers (see also Appendix IX).

A word of caution

Questions must not be asked that could be seen as prejudiced. I ran a tribunal case some years ago for a doctor who was claiming sex discrimination. She had been denied (self-employed) work after she became pregnant with her third child. The reason for refusing her emerged when her medical manager conceded that he 'may' have used the phrase 'Are you sure you are going to be able to cope?' The tribunal considered that this almost certainly would not have been said had the doctor been a man. It was therefore evidence of a discriminatory assumption, and for this among other reasons they upheld the doctor's case.

Asking open questions can provide the employer with the basis for a workplace discussion and can avoid suggesting discrimination. A useful exercise is to ask employees about *their* plans and aims over:

- the short term
- the medium term
- the long term.

This will help to organise training and development, and appropriate succession plans. It must not just be limited to older workers. It also allows employees to focus on their future goals.

When discussing future plans, an employer should consider the skills the workforce possesses and how best to deploy these. Holding such discussions could help match an employer's needs with employee aspirations and this should benefit the practice.

The outcome of workplace discussions should be recorded and held for as long as there is a business need for doing so. It would be good practice, build trust and aid transparency to give a copy of the discussion record to the employee.

Poor performance

If an employee is performing poorly the employer should discuss this with him or her to establish the causes. Failure to address poor performance in older employees because, or in the expectation that, they will be leaving soon to draw their pension, or that it may be seen to be undignified, may well be discriminatory. Employers should avoid falling into the stereotype that poor performance is more likely to be associated with older workers.

Establishing the reasons for poor performance, setting improvement periods and agreeing on what training and development would help the employee meet the work expectations are all key to managing this element.

Nothing should be done that would suggest that discriminatory assumptions are held. (See Appendix VI on the Equality Act 2010 for details.)

Poor, or reduced, performance will generally be manifested as a lack of capability. Occasionally it will be misconduct. Employers should also ensure that they comply with the disability discrimination elements of the Equality Act as follows.

Disability

- The Equality Act 2010 provides disabled people with protection from discrimination in the workplace.
- Employers must make reasonable adjustments to accommodate an employee with a disability.
- Disabled employees are protected from harassment at work.
- Employers should have polices in place to prevent discrimination.

It is unlawful to discriminate against employees because of a physical or mental disability, or to fail to make reasonable adjustments to accommodate an employee with a disability.

Under the act a person is classified as disabled if he or she has a physical or mental impairment that has a substantial and long-term effect on the person's ability to carry out normal day-to-day activities.[1]

Day-to-day activities include things such as using a telephone, reading a book or using public transport.

The work provisions of the act require employers not to:

- directly discriminate against a person because of his or her actual or perceived disability, or because the person associates with a disabled person
- treat a disabled person less favourably for a reason related to his or her impairment, unless that treatment can be justified. For example an employer may reject someone who has a severe back problem where the job entails heavy lifting
- have procedures, policy or practices that, although applicable to all employees, disproportionately disadvantage those who share a particular disability, unless these can be justified
- fail to make reasonable adjustments in the recruitment and employment of disabled people. This can include, for example, adjustments to recruitment and selection procedures, to terms and conditions of employment, and to working arrangements and physical changes to the premises or equipment
- treat an employee unfairly who has made or supported a complaint about discrimination because of disability.

Disabled employees are also protected from harassment. Harassment is unwanted conduct related to disability that has the purpose or effect of violating an individual's dignity or creating an intimidating, hostile, degrading, humiliating or offensive environment for that individual.

Practices should ensure they have policies in place that are designed to prevent discrimination in:

- recruitment and selection
- determining pay
- training and development
- selection for promotion
- grievances and discipline (including countering bullying and harassment).

If an employee has a disability that is making it difficult for him or her to work, a practice should consider what reasonable adjustments it can make in the workplace to help, or schedule an interview with the employee to discuss what can be done to support him or her. This could be as simple as supplying an adequate, ergonomic chair or power-assisted piece of equipment. Reasonable adjustments also include re-deployment to a different type of work if necessary.

If an employee feels they been discriminated against, they may bring a claim to an employment tribunal. However, they should talk to their employer first to try to sort out the matter informally, in order to minimise the negative effects on all parties involved.

Capability

This is defined as a skill or aptitude, health or some other physical or mental quality. That is, it is something inherent in the individual, albeit something that can be acquired. An employer will need to determine what it is. In any event, standards must be set, and these must be made known to the employee.

You should consider the extent of the poor performance. Is it fundamental to the job or can it be managed and what has been the previous performance?

The procedure to use will depend on the reasons for poor performance as follows.

Skills

You should work through the following questions.

- Has the employee received the appropriate training? If not, organise it.
- If yes, then why is competence not being demonstrated?
- Is further training required? If so, arrange this and then arrange a follow-up meeting.

Aptitude

Does the employee have an aptitude that is not being used? If so, why not? Is it a case of misconduct?

Health

The following section on managing sickness absence shows the different approaches required.

A discussion with the employee will be required before embarking on disciplinary procedures. This would seek to identify the root causes of the poor performance and clear out of the way any action that needs to be taken by the employer, e.g. organising training. Only then should the formal procedure be started.

Disciplinary procedures can, and should, be used in the following situations:

- a refusal to agree to a reasonable request to undergo training
- a wilful refusal to apply skills or apply a known aptitude
- a refusal to agree to a reasonable request to change working methods
- a refusal to follow a practice rule.

Misconduct

This relates to *behaviour* and generally involves a breach of rules, or perhaps the breach of an implied term of the employment contract (see Chapter 2). As such, technically it constitutes a breach of contract. The disciplinary procedures may therefore be used, starting with early stages for relatively minor breaches, and working through them if the misconduct continues or is repeated.

If the breach of contract is held to be gross misconduct it is advisable to invoke the final stage that could lead to dismissal, because failure to comply with some of the implied terms (e.g. to obey reasonable and lawful instructions) constitutes a repudiation of the contract on the part of the employee.

In cases of continuing, minor misconduct the disciplinary procedures should be used as they stand. That is, starting at the first level if counselling fails to resolve matters – a verbal warning and progressing through written warnings as necessary.

For managing a formal disciplinary hearing see Chapter 3.

Appraisal

Appraisal schemes should not be used as a disciplinary mechanism to deal with poor performers but it is important to establish a procedure for informing employees in writing of unsatisfactory appraisals. The consequences of failure to meet the required standards should be explained to the employee and confirmed in writing.

For those practices with no appraisal scheme, self-appraisal could be useful. For an example of a self-appraisal framework see Appendix VIII.

Managing sickness absence

To effectively manage staff absence a practice must first measure it. Next, the appropriate procedure should be deployed, depending on the type of problem (if there is one), be it short-term sickness, long-term sickness or unauthorised absence. Practice policy on absence should be copied to staff. Further, it is strongly advised that before introducing any new measure staff should be consulted.

Some practices may feel inhibited about taking action on sickness absence, something that is beyond the control of most employees. If so, take heart from an Employment Appeal Tribunal judgment in 2014 that ruled in a disability case that among other things:

> it was legitimate for an employer to aim for consistent attendance at work; and the carefully considered final written warning *was plainly a proportionate means of achieving that legitimate aim* [emphasis added].[2]

Dismissal is not being advocated here, but reducing sickness absence is. Consistent attendance is held to be a legitimate aim. Provided a reasonable procedure is used, a proportionate means is being used. Set out below are the different procedures to be used for different kinds of absence.

First, though, some benchmarking information: each year the Chartered Institute of Personnel and Development (CIPD) carries out an annual survey of days lost to sickness by their member organisations. In 2014 its analysis was based on replies from 518 organisations across the UK employing 1.4 million employees.

Table 4.1: CIPD survey of sickness absence – October 2014

	Public sector	*Private sector*	*Average*
Length*	7.9 days	5.5 days	6.6 days
Cost*	£914	£520	£609

*Per employee per year.

Source: taken from the CIPD Absence management 2014 survey report produced in partnership with Simplyhealth and used with permission.[3]

The CIPD survey reveals that overall there has been a fall in absence levels this year by one day per employee to 6.6 days.[3] Public sector absence has also fallen by almost a day, although, at 7.9 days per employee, this figure is still significantly higher than in the private sector.

The survey found, interestingly, that absence levels tend to increase with organisation size, regardless of sector.

When asked, the most common *management change* reported was to develop line manager capability to manage absence. Other common changes included introducing a new or revised absence policy, reinforcing an existing one and introducing or revising monitoring procedures. There was also an increased focus this year on attendance. Only a minority from any sector, however, have introduced or revised an attendance incentive scheme.

The most common approaches to short-term absence, as in previous years, focus on procedures to monitor and deter absence, including return-to-work interviews, trigger mechanisms to review attendance, disciplinary procedures for unacceptable absence and giving sickness absence information to line managers.

Approaches used to manage long-term absence are also similar to previous years. Return-to-work interviews remain the most common method used, followed by Occupational Health involvement, risk assessments to aid return to work and giving sickness absence information to line managers.

Action

The lesson to take from the CIPD survey, I believe, is that a public sector employee will take on average around *eight days of sickness absence per year*. Accordingly, if your practice shows average absence levels close to this, you do not have a problem. You probably need do nothing more than you usually do about absence management.

If, on the other hand, your absence levels are averaging far above eight days per employee, you *do* have a problem and you should start managing it.

If you cannot say what your average sickness absence is per employee then you need to implement a record system that will tell you what the figures are. This should be part of a practice absence policy.

Absence records

It is vital for practices to know their absence levels, and possibly how they compare with other practices. This may require setting up a recording system, ideally on a spreadsheet, to facilitate the analysis.

There are no legal requirements regarding absence records as such. However, if a member of staff is dismissed and a practice has failed to keep proper records, it is more likely that an employee would succeed in an employment tribunal application for unfair dismissal.

A record system should show how much time is lost; how often individual employees are absent; and what type of absence type they have (short- or long-term, or unauthorised). For specimen records see Appendix VII.

If the records are kept on a spreadsheet it is possible to keep a running total of the absence of all practice staff throughout the year, and this can be transferred automatically to the practice record. Using the spreadsheet formulas it is then an easy matter to calculate practice totals, and the average for each category of absence for the whole practice.

For more information try googling 'spreadsheet formulas'.

Specifically, the following should be done:

- keep accurate attendance records, ideally on a spreadsheet, which show individual instances of absence, together with duration and reason
- ensure that records can be easily analysed by month or year
- ensure that absence measurement figures show the scale and nature of the situation, whether there is high absence and which of the main categories of absence are involved – short-term certified or uncertified sickness, long-term sickness or unauthorised absence and lateness.

In what follows:

- short-term absence is taken as lasting under four weeks
- long-term absence is four weeks or more.

These two categories demand different treatment.

Putting in place policies and procedures to manage sickness absence and return to work need not be difficult – there is already an established body of good practice to build upon. You may already have some elements of a policy in place but it is worth reviewing them for their effectiveness.

In particular, you might need to take a fresh look at how you:

- record, monitor and measure sickness absence
- train your supervisors or team leaders in managing sickness absence and return to work
- keep in contact with absent employees and plan with them for their return to work
- access professional advice and treatment to help your employees.

Clearly, a practice should tailor its absence policy to the causes of absence among staff. This requires a diagnostic approach to those causes, including paying due regard to disability rights (see pp. 24–6) and, where necessary, accidents.

Reduce high absence levels by paying special attention to:

- employment relations
- communications; induction and training
- health and safety
- working conditions
- job design.

Deal with short-term certificated or un-certificated sickness by:

- having a policy on the provision of certificates to cover sickness absence
- 'interviewing' employees on their return to work
- seeking explanations where there is a high level of short-term absence
- arranging Occupational Health medicals where necessary
- ensuring employees are told if their level of absence is putting their job at risk
- taking disciplinary action if a high level of absence continues.

Disciplinary action should be taken as with any other (initially) minor breach, with targets set for attendance over, say, the next two months. Review this after the agreed period unless the employee goes over his or her target before then. If he or she does, hold the review immediately on the employee's return. If necessary set a new review period and review this as before. If there is no improvement use the practice disciplinary procedure to escalate the level of warning, to the final stage eventually if no improvement is forthcoming.

Remember the *legitimate aim of consistent attendance at work* referred to above. Failure to attend regularly for work is a breach of the implied term (to attend regularly for work) and in the long term, subject to warning, may justify dismissal. You do not start with this, but you may end up with it.

Deal with long-term sickness by:

- discussing the problem with the employee concerned, and his or her representative
- seeking medical opinions from the employee's GP and Occupational Health
- considering whether the job can be covered by other employees or temporary replacements and how long the job can be kept open (but be aware of the requirements of disability discrimination legislation [see pp. 24–6])
- considering alternative work or working arrangements
- dismissing only after *all of the above* followed by consultation with the employee and his or her representative.

Deal with unauthorised absence or lateness by:

- requiring absent employees to phone in by a given time on each day of absence

- ensuring that the supervisor or practice manager has an informal talk with the employee on the day after an absence to seek an explanation
- taking disciplinary action if the unexplained absence continues.

Bullying and harassment

Bullying may be characterised as offensive, intimidating, malicious or insulting behaviour, an abuse or misuse of power through means intended to undermine, humiliate, denigrate or injure the recipient.

Harassment, in general terms, is unwanted conduct affecting the dignity of men and women in the workplace. It may be related to age, sex, race, disability, religion, nationality or any other personal characteristic of the individual. It may be persistent or it may be an isolated incident. The key is that the actions or comments are viewed as demeaning and are unacceptable *to the recipient.*

Bullying or harassment may be by an individual against an individual (perhaps by someone in a position of authority such as a manager or supervisor) or it may involve groups of people. It may be obvious or it may be hidden.

Examples of bullying or harassing behaviour include:

- overbearing supervision or other misuse of power or position
- deliberately undermining a competent employee by overloading and constant criticism
- making threats or comments about job security without foundation
- ridiculing or demeaning someone – picking on a person or setting him or her up to fail
- unfair treatment
- preventing individuals progressing by intentionally blocking promotion or training opportunities
- spreading malicious rumours, or insulting a colleague by word or behaviour
- copying memos that are critical about someone to others who do not need to know
- exclusion or victimisation
- unwelcome sexual advances – touching, standing too close and the display of offensive materials.

Bullying and harassment are not necessarily face to face. They may also occur in written communications, emails and phone calls.

Bullying and harassment make someone feel anxious and humiliated. Feelings of anger and frustration at being unable to cope may be triggered. Some people may try to retaliate in some way. Others may become frightened and de-motivated. Stress, loss of self-confidence and loss of self-esteem caused by harassment or bullying can lead to job insecurity, illness, absence from work and even resignation. Almost always job performance is affected and relations in the workplace suffer.

The legal position

Employers are responsible for preventing bullying and harassing behaviour; they have a duty of care. It is in their interests to make it clear to everyone that such behaviour will not be tolerated – the costs to the practice may include poor employee relations, low morale, inefficiency and potentially the loss of staff.

A policy statement to all staff about the standards of behaviour expected can make it easier for all individuals to be fully aware of their responsibilities to others. The disciplinary procedures should be used where staff transgress.

Unfair dismissal

If the mutual trust and confidence between employer and employee is broken – for example, through bullying and harassment at work – then an employee may resign and claim constructive dismissal on the grounds of breach of contract. Employers are usually responsible in law for the acts of their employees.

Health and safety

Breach of contract may also include the failure to protect an employee's health and safety at work. Under legislation employers are responsible for the health, safety and welfare at work of all employees (see Chapter 6).

The Health and Safety Executive's advice to managers considers that bullying is primarily an industrial relations issue and as such should be dealt with by an employer's internal grievance and disciplinary procedures long before it becomes a risk to employees' health.[4] However, it is recognised that relationships at work (including negative relationships involving bullying and harassment) can be a source of work-related stress.

Stress is defined as *the adverse reaction a person has to excessive pressure or other types of demand placed upon them.* In tackling work-related stress employers are reminded that looking after the health of employees includes taking steps to make sure that employees do not suffer stress-related illness *as a result of work.*

Legal remedies

There is no *specific* legal protection against bullying. Employees would need to rely on general contractual and employment law principles. Workplace bullying will often involve a breach of an implied term or condition of employment, most obviously the mutual obligation of trust and confidence. This includes the obligation not to allow staff to be humiliated, intimidated or degraded. A breach of contract would result from a failure to treat staff with dignity and consideration, and a failure to deal with employees' complaints and treat them with sufficient gravity.

Failure to provide reasonable support to enable a worker to carry out his or her duties without disruption or harassment from fellow workers would also be a breach of the implied terms of trust and confidence. Other relevant implied terms will be the obligation to provide a safe workplace, and safe and competent colleagues.

Harassment

The Equality Act 2010 uses a single definition of harassment to cover the relevant protected characteristics (see Appendix VI). Employees can complain of behaviour that they find offensive even if it is not directed at them.

An employer is *no longer* legally liable for harassment by someone who does not work for that employer, such as a patient or a contractor. However, all practices should have a policy that encourages employees to let them know if they are being harassed in this way so that the practice can take steps to prevent it from happening again.

Discrimination and harassment

It is not possible to make a direct complaint to an employment tribunal about bullying. However, employees may bring complaints under the law covering discrimination and harassment.

What can the employer do?

Bullying and harassment are often clear cut but sometimes people may be unsure whether or not the way they are being treated is acceptable. If this applies there are a number of things to consider, including:

- has there been a change of management or organisational style that just needs time to adjust to – perhaps because of a new manager or new work requirements?
- is there a policy statement that covers the situation?
- do staff feel able to talk over their worries with the practice manager?

- is it possible to agree changes to workload or ways of working that make things easier?
- if behaviour is perceived as bullying or harassing consider use of disciplinary procedures.

If any of the above applies, an employer would be expected to take appropriate action. This should include an investigation and action taken to prevent any harassment that has occurred, including disciplinary action if necessary.

Remember the duty of care – employers are responsible for the health, safety and welfare at work of all employees. This will generally require an investigation into complaints and action taken to prevent any harassment that has occurred, including disciplinary action against the perpetrator if appropriate.

Employment scenarios

1. A patient has complained in writing about the attitude of one of the receptionists, and colleagues have commented informally about her. She was spoken to about this around a year ago.

    What should you do now?

2. One of your clerical staff is having problems coping with the records system. At her appraisal she says that she has never got used to computers and prefers the old days when everything was done by hand.

    How would you deal with this?

References

1. Equality Act 2010. www.legislation.gov.uk/ukpga/2010/15/contents [accessed 13 November 2014].
2. www.employmentappeals.gov.uk/public/search.aspx and search for UKEAT/0107/14/KN.
3. Chartered Institute of Personnel and Development. *Absence management 2014*. London: CIPD, 2014. www.cipd.co.uk/hr-resources/survey-reports/absence-management-2014.aspx [accessed 13 November 2014].
4. Health and Safety Executive. Bullying & harassment: advice for managers. www.hse.gov.uk/stress/furtheradvice/informationonbullying.htm [accessed 13 November 2014].

5

Terminating the contract

Ending the contract
Notice periods and pay
Dismissal
Handling dismissal in the workplace
Constructive dismissal
Redundancy
Employment scenarios

Ending the contract

An employment contract can be terminated at any time by either party. It could be a resignation or dismissal, redundancy or retirement, all with or without notice. For notice to be effective it should be in writing and specify the date of termination.

Notice periods and pay

- Both the employee and employer are normally entitled to a minimum period of notice on termination of employment.
- Notice periods should be one of the main terms and conditions of employment and included in the written contract.
- All forms of notice should be in writing to clarify that it is the termination of employment.
- In most cases employees should be paid their normal pay during the notice period.
- Normal notice applies when employment is being terminated due to redundancy.

> **Box 5.1: Unfair dismissal in an employment tribunal**
>
> From the Employment Rights Act 1996 section 98, as amended.
>
> The dismissal of an employee is unfair if the *reason does not relate* to the following.
>
> 1. The *capability* or qualifications of the employee for performing work of the kind which he or she was employed to do. [Capability means his or her ability assessed by reference to skill, aptitude, health or any other physical or mental quality. Qualifications mean any degree, diploma or other academic, technical or professional qualification relevant to the position which he or she held.]
> 2. The *conduct* of the employee.
> 3. The employee was *redundant*.
> 4. The employee *could not continue* to work in the position that he or she held without contravention (either on the employee's part or on that of his or her employer) of a duty or restriction imposed by or under an enactment.
> 5. *Some other substantial reason* of a kind such as to justify the dismissal of an employee holding the position which he or she held.
>
> *and/or*
>
> the employer acted unreasonably in dismissing in the circumstances.
>
> This latter will depend on:
> 1. The size and administrative resources of the employer's undertaking, *and*
> 2. Equity and the substantial merits of the case.

Statutory minimum periods of notice

After one month employees are entitled to one week's notice for the first two years in their job. This rises to three weeks' notice after three years' service and by one week for each subsequent year of service up to a maximum of 12 weeks' notice after 12 or more years' service. Any notice periods written into the contract that are longer will override the statutory requirements.

Dismissal

In carrying out the dismissal both the *reason* for the dismissal and the employer's *reasonableness* will be scrutinised by a tribunal if the former employee makes a claim.

How reasonableness is judged

The following are examples of the sort of issues considered by tribunals when determining the question of an employer's reasonableness:

- whether dismissal was an action within the 'band of reasonable responses' for the employer to take in the circumstances
- in conduct cases, did the employer have reasonable grounds for believing that the employee had done the act concerned?
- had the employer carried out a reasonable investigation?
- had the employer followed its own procedure?
- did the employee know the allegations against him or her and was the employee allowed to put his or her side of the story
- was the employee allowed the right to be accompanied at the disciplinary hearing?
- in capability cases, was the employee warned and given a reasonable time to improve, with appropriate training, if necessary
- in long-term sickness cases, was the employee consulted and his or her doctor asked for a view as to when the employee could be expected to return and his or her ability to do the job on return?

Additionally, in assessing reasonableness the employment tribunal will take due regard to such things as the employee's length of service, the size of the employer and consistency of treatment.

So both dismissal reason and employer reasonableness is important here.

Reason for dismissal

There are currently five situations where a dismissal will potentially be fair (see Box 5.1). This indicates those reasons that are *not unfair*. The first three are the most common advanced at a tribunal, while the first two are most relevant to general practice – capability and conduct. If an employee is dismissed, one of these two reasons will invariably be the reason why. So far, so good. Next we come to the employer's handling of the dismissal.

Reasonableness

Essentially, to show this an employer will have to demonstrate that an appropriate *procedure* was used. To ensure that the correct procedure is followed the best source of advice is the Acas Code, summarised in Appendix IV.

The practice disciplinary procedures, which should be attached to the employment contract, must be consistent with the Acas Code and they must be followed as appropriate. The employee could be provided with a copy at the time disciplinary action is taken, should this be necessary.

Compensation payable

Although tribunals have the power to order reinstatement and re-engagement after a finding of unfair dismissal, this power is seldom used.

Compensation in an unfair dismissal case is made up of a basic award and a compensatory award. The basic award is calculated in the same way as a redundancy payment and is related to age and length of service. The compensatory award is just that: it aims to compensate the former employee for estimated *future* losses.

The Employment Tribunal service statistics for the 12 months to March 2014 show that while the statutory maximum is £76,574, the average compensation *actually awarded* for unfair dismissal was £11,813.

Handling dismissal in the workplace

To avoid potentially expensive tribunal cases the Acas Code should be followed. For serious misconduct this covers the following steps. For further advice see Acas.[1]

1. *Investigate in order to establish the facts of each case.* It is important to carry out all necessary investigations of potential disciplinary matters without unreasonable delay to establish the facts of the case. In some cases this will require the holding of an investigatory meeting with the employee before proceeding to any disciplinary hearing.

2. *Inform the employee of the problem – in writing* – and explain that a meeting is required. If it is decided that there is a disciplinary case to answer, the employee should be notified of this in writing. This notification should contain sufficient information about the alleged misconduct or poor performance and its possible consequences to enable the employee to prepare to answer the case at a disciplinary meeting.

3. *Hold a meeting with the employee to discuss the problem* – not necessarily the same day. At the meeting the employer should explain the complaint against the employee and go through the evidence that has been gathered. The employee should be allowed to set out his or her case and answer any allegations that have been made. The employee should also be given a reasonable opportunity to ask questions, present evidence and call relevant witnesses. He or she should also be given an opportunity to raise points about any information provided by witnesses.

4. *Allow the employee to be accompanied at the meeting by a colleague or union official.* Employees have a statutory right to be accompanied by a companion where the disciplinary meeting could result in formal action. The chosen companion may be a fellow worker, a trade union representative or an official employed by a trade union.

5. *Decide on appropriate action – which should be proportionate and timely.* After the meeting decide whether or not disciplinary or any other action is justified and inform the employee accordingly in writing. Where misconduct is confirmed or the employee is found to be performing unsatisfactorily it is usual to give the employee a written warning. A further act of misconduct or failure to improve performance within a set period would normally result in a final written warning. If an employee's first misconduct or unsatisfactory performance is sufficiently serious, it may be appropriate to move directly to a final written warning. This might occur where the employee's actions have had, or are liable to have, a serious or harmful impact on the practice.

6. *Provide employees with an opportunity to appeal.* Where an employee feels that disciplinary action taken against him or her is wrong or unjust, the employee should be able to appeal against the decision. Appeals should be heard without unreasonable delay and ideally at an agreed time and place. Employees should let employers know the grounds for their appeal in writing. The appeal should be dealt with impartially. Wherever possible, it should be dealt with by a manager who has not previously been involved in the case. Employees have a statutory right to be accompanied at appeal hearings.

Appeal against dismissal

The last needs careful management because an appeal may rectify any previous procedural errors. It may also provide, should it be needed, further evidence of reasonableness.

The *decision* itself to dismiss following an appeal is not something for the partners to delegate. However, they can delegate the *hearing* of an appeal and ask for a recommendation regarding the ultimate decision.

My advice is to establish an advisory panel of individuals who have not previously been involved in the decision. Members might include: the practice accountant; the Local Medical Committee secretary; a nominee from the trust's HR department; or a partner. If such a panel is set up it should be an odd number, to avoid the possibility of a tied vote.

Constructive dismissal

This is when the employee (*ostensibly*) makes the first move.

Constructive dismissal occurs when an employee is forced to leave his or her job because of the employer's conduct. In order to prove constructive dismissal, an employee needs to show that his or her employer has committed a serious *breach of contract*, that the employee felt forced to leave because of that breach, and that he or she had done nothing to suggest the employee accepted this breach or change in employment conditions.

Such claims can often be difficult to prove, but if successful they can give rise to damages for wrongful dismissal in a civil action. Also, if an employee has more than two years' service, he or she is entitled to bring a claim for unfair dismissal in a tribunal action.

So what can employers do to guard against such claims? On its website Acas offers some hints for employers on avoiding constructive dismissal claims, as follows.

First, it is essential to have effective procedures governing performance management, discipline, and grievance and dismissal. It is also important to communicate these procedures to staff and ensure that they are implanted consistently and fairly.

Second, it is strongly advised to try to nip any problems in the bud. Make sure that any issues are addressed promptly, and work together with the member of staff concerned to resolve any problems before they escalate.

Third, in a case where a resigning employee is thought likely to be planning a claim for constructive dismissal, an employer might want to contact him or her in writing. The employer should ask the employee to reconsider his or her decision to resign and confirm the decision in writing, or invite the employee in for a discussion.

Box 5.2: Constructive dismissal – the law

A termination of the contract *by the employee* will constitute a dismissal within the act if he or she is entitled to so terminate because of the employer's conduct. However, it is not enough for the employee to leave merely because the employer has acted unreasonably. The employer's conduct must amount to a *breach of the contract of employment*. Further, a constructive dismissal is not necessarily *unfair* and the employer's actions will be considered in the light of a reasonable employer in the circumstances.

For an employee to claim constructive dismissal, four conditions must be met:

1. There must be a breach of contract by the employer, either actual or anticipatory
2. The breach must be sufficiently important to justify resigning, or else it must be a last straw

3. The employee must leave in response to the breach and not for some other, unconnected reason
4. The employee must not delay too long in terminating the contract, otherwise he or she may be deemed to have waived the breach and agreed to vary the contract.

In many cases, a constructive dismissal claim will arise following the breach of an *implied term* of the contract, principally the duty of trust and confidence. In a (non-legal) sense this relates to whether or not the employer has behaved *reasonably* towards the employee.

Other implied terms include the duty of cooperation on the part of the employer and fairness in disciplinary sanctions.

Waiving the breach. Where the conduct by the employer constitutes the unilateral imposition of a new term (e.g. a reduction in wages) the employee may by his or her conduct be treated as having *agreed* to the variation. Thereafter the conduct of the employer does not constitute a breach at all. In one case, an employee was precluded from claiming constructive dismissal because he had remained for four weeks after it had become clear that his grievance would not be remedied. Consequently he was taken to have affirmed the contract.

There is no fixed time within which the employee must make up his or her mind. It depends upon all the circumstances, including length of service, the nature of the breach, and whether the employee has protested at the change, i.e. used the grievance procedure.

Where a number of terms are changed in a contract, e.g. a new job in another location, an employee can justifiably argue that he or she needs time to assess the new terms. However, where the breach does not involve new terms being imposed, but instead consists of a simple act such as unlawful suspension, or failure to make a bonus payment, the courts might require the employee to make up his or her mind more quickly.

In one case the Employment Appeal Tribunal held that a month was *too long* to remain at work where six months had already elapsed since the alleged repudiatory act occurred. However, it was said that a month from the initial breach might not be fatal. If the employee specifically makes clear his or her objections while continuing to work, a longer period may elapse without a waiver being held to have occurred.

For information about employment tribunals – procedures and compensation – see Appendix IV.

Redundancy

What is redundancy?

Redundancy is a fair form of dismissal, providing that the contract of employment is terminated in a reasonable and fair manner.

When does redundancy occur?

Redundancy arises when a practice ceases its activities (or is about to cease), or the number of employees required to carry out a particular job ceases or diminishes. For example, abolition of fundholding arrangements meant that the need to have staff working on fund management ceased. In such circumstances a redundancy situation was created.

Why might the number of employees diminish?

- Where there is less work.
- Where the workforce is re-organised.
- When changes in conditions mean the old job is quite different from the new one.
- When work is contracted out.

What is the employer required to do?

The employer is required to act 'in a fair and reasonable manner'. This requires, first, consultation with staff about the need for redundancies, and next the establishment of *criteria for selecting* who is to be made redundant. The practice must then identify the 'pool' of employees to whom the selection criteria will apply.

The practice must also consider if there is any suitable alternative employment (within the practice) that can be offered to potentially redundant staff. If this is not considered, the redundancy may be deemed to be an unfair dismissal. This can occur if reasonable procedures are not followed, even when posts are in fact redundant.

Consultation with the employees concerned is essential.

What selection criteria can be used?

The criteria must be objective and not biased against any groups (see protected characteristics in the Equality Act 2010 in Appendix VI). They can include one or a combination of the following:

- volunteers
- skills, experience and qualifications
- standard of work performance
- attendance, fitness and health (but beware discrimination on grounds of disability)
- disciplinary record

- last in, first out (but beware age bias).

Box 5.3: How much redundancy pay can staff expect?

For those staff *with two years' service*,* the statutory scheme provides for:
- *0.5 weeks' pay*** for each complete year when the employee was under 22 years of age

plus
- *one week's pay*** for each complete year when the employee was between 22 and 41 years

plus
- *1.5 week's pay*** for each complete year in which the employee was aged 41 or more.

Redundancy payments are made in a lump sum and are tax free up to £30,000.

* Employees can only count a maximum of 20 years' service and **'weekly pay' is subject to an upper limit of £464 a week (from 6 April 2014).

Agenda for Change redundancy terms

For reference, these are as follows. Staff who are made redundant receive one month's pay per year of reckonable service, with a maximum of 24 months' pay (only full years of reckonable service can be counted). For more information see the NHS Employers website.[2]

Employment scenarios

1. The senior partner tells you that one of the receptionists has sworn at him in the course of an argument and he 'wants her out'.

   How do you respond?

2. A fortnight before a receptionist is due to go on holiday she asks if she can bring it forward so that she can fly with friends. Because of staff shortages you have to refuse. The receptionist then goes sick for the week before her holidays.

   How do you deal with this?

References
1. Acas. *Discipline and grievances at work: the Acas guide*. London: Acas, 2014. www.acas.org.uk/media/pdf/l/g/Discipline-and-grievances-Acas-guide.pdf [accessed 13 November 2014].

2. NHS Employers. NHS redundancy arrangements – Section 16. www.nhsemployers.org/your-workforce/pay-and-reward/nhs-terms-and-conditions/nhs-terms-and-conditions-of-service-handbook/nhs-redundancy-arrangements [accessed 13 November 2014].

6

Specific legal issues

Statutory rights
Maternity rights
Paternity leave and pay
Equality rights
Statutory leave entitlement
Parental leave
Flexible working
Part-time employees
Temporary contracts
Health and safety
Employment scenarios

Statutory rights

Statutory employment rights are incorporated into employment contracts by law. The only requirement is that the individual contract holder is an employee within the meaning of the act (as opposed to a 'worker'). For more on the status of workers see Chapter 1.

Under the Employment Rights Act an 'employee' means an individual who has entered into or works under a contract of employment and 'contract of employment' means a contract of service or apprenticeship, whether express – oral or in writing – or implied.

Box 6.1: **Employee not worker**

Someone who works for a practice is probably an employee if most of the following are true. He or she:
- is required to work regularly unless he or she is on leave – e.g. holiday, sick leave or maternity leave
- is required to do a minimum number of hours and expects to be paid for time worked
- has a manager or supervisor who is responsible for his or her workload, saying when a piece of work should be finished and how it should be done
- cannot send someone else to do his or her work
- has tax and National Insurance contributions deducted from his or her wages by the practice
- gets paid holiday
- is entitled to contractual or Statutory Sick Pay, and Maternity or Paternity Pay
- can join the practice's pension scheme
- is bound by the practice's disciplinary and grievance procedures
- works at the practice's premises or at an address specified by the practice
- has a contract that sets out redundancy procedures
- has materials, tools and equipment provided by the practice for his or her work
- only works for the practice, or if he or she does have another job, it's completely different from his or her work for the practice
- has a contract, statement of terms and conditions or offer letter (which can be described as an 'employment contract') that uses terms like 'employer' and 'employee'.

Source: adapted from Gov.uk.[1]

Maternity rights

Maternity leave and pay

- Pregnant employees have the right to 52 weeks' maternity leave.
- Thirty-nine weeks could be paid, which may be Statutory Maternity Pay (SMP), Maternity Allowance or Contractual Maternity Pay (contractual pay may be more than statutory pay or could be paid for longer than 39 weeks, but this will depend on the contract terms).
- During maternity leave employee and employer can agree to have up to ten 'keeping-in-touch days'.

- Paid reasonable time off is available for antenatal care.
- The employee has the right to return to her original job or a suitable alternative.

A pregnant employee has the right to both 26 weeks of Ordinary Maternity Leave as well as 26 weeks of Additional Maternity Leave. To qualify for maternity leave, an employee must tell her employer by the end of the 15th week before the expected week of childbirth

- that she is pregnant
- the expected week of childbirth, by means of a medical certificate if requested
- the date she intends to start maternity leave. This can normally be any date that is no earlier that the beginning of the 11th week before the expected week of childbirth up to the birth.

Once notification has been given to the employer, the latter must then write to the employee, within 28 days of her notification, setting out her return date. The employee must give eight weeks' notice if she wishes to change the return date.

All pregnant employees are entitled to reasonable time off with pay for antenatal care undertaken on the advice of a registered medical practitioner, which may include relaxation classes and parent-craft classes. Except for the first appointment, employees should show the employer, if requested, an appointment card or other documents showing that an appointment has been made.

Shared Parental Leave

A new right will enable eligible mothers, fathers, partners and adopters to choose how to share time off work after their child is born or placed.[2] This could mean that the mother or adopter shares some of the leave with her partner, perhaps returning to work for part of the time and then resuming leave at a later date.

The regulations came into force in December 2014. The options to use the new Shared Parental Leave rights will apply for parents who meet the eligibility criteria, where a baby is due to be born on or after 5 April 2015, or for children who are placed for adoption on or after that date.

A summary of the key points is available on the Gov.uk website.[3]

Statutory Maternity Pay

SMP will be payable if the employee has been employed continuously for at least 26 weeks ending with the 15th week before the expected week of childbirth, and has an average weekly earnings at least equal to the lower earnings limit for National Insurance contributions. See Appendix II.

SMP is payable for 39 weeks; for the first six weeks it is paid at 90% of the average weekly earning. The following 33 weeks will be paid at the SMP rate or 90% of the average weekly earnings, whichever is the lower. The SMP rate from April 2014 is £138.18 per week; the standard rate for SMP is reviewed every April. Gov.uk has an online SMP Ready Reckoner.[4]

Maternity allowance

Women who do not qualify for SMP may be entitled to Maternity Allowance,[5] paid by Jobcentre Plus, for up to 39 weeks. To qualify, they must have been employed or self-employed for 26 weeks out of the 66 weeks before the expected week of childbirth.

Also paid by Jobcentre Plus is the Sure Start Maternity Grant,[6] currently £500 for first-time mothers and those on certain benefits. This must be claimed (by the mother) before the baby is three months' old.

Employee rights when on leave

Employee rights are not usually affected when employees take maternity, paternity, adoption or parental leave, and some employees can work up to ten paid days during their leave.

Employees whose baby is due or who adopt a child on or after 5 April 2015 may be entitled to take Shared Parental Leave.[2]

Keeping in touch days

Employees can work up to ten days during their maternity, adoption or additional paternity leave. These days are called 'keeping-in-touch days'. Keeping in touch days are optional – both the employee and employer need to agree to them.

The type of work and pay employees get should be agreed before they come into work. The employee's right to maternity, adoption or additional paternity leave and pay is not affected by taking keeping in touch days.

Terms and conditions protection

Normally, the employment terms and conditions are protected and employees are entitled to any pay rises and improvements in terms and conditions given during the leave.

Pension contributions usually stop if a period of leave is unpaid, unless the contract says otherwise. For example, this applies during unpaid periods of maternity leave or parental leave.

Employees continue to build up holiday entitlement and can take any holiday they've accrued before or after the leave.

Returning to work

Employees have the right to return to their job if they take only:

- Ordinary Maternity or Ordinary Adoption Leave
- Ordinary Paternity Leave
- Additional Paternity Leave
- four weeks or less of parental leave.

The rules are different if the employee takes:

- Additional Maternity or Additional Adoption Leave
- more than four weeks of parental leave.

In this situation, employees have the right to their job or a similar job (if it's not possible to give them their old job). Similar means the job has the same or better terms and conditions. If the employee unreasonably refuses to take the similar job the employer can take this as his or her resignation.

Redundancy

Employees have the same redundancy rights as their colleagues while on maternity, adoption, paternity or parental leave.

Employees have the right to be offered any suitable alternative job if they are selected for redundancy (even if other colleagues are more suitable for the role) while on maternity, adoption or paternity leave.

An employee can only be made redundant if the employer can clearly justify doing it, e.g. a part of the business closes and everyone in that section is made redundant. There are other rules when making staff redundant (see Chapter 5).

NB pregnancy and maternity are together one of the 'protected characteristics' under the Equality Act 2010 (see Appendix VI) so any discrimination on these grounds is unlawful.

Paternity leave and pay

An employee who is a father-to-be, or who will share the responsibility with a partner for bringing up a child, may have the right to Statutory Paternity Leave and Pay. This includes those who are adopting a child.

Paternity leave is available to employees who:

- have or expect to have responsibility for the child's upbringing
- are the biological father of the child, or who are the mother's husband or partner (including same-sex relationships)
- have worked continuously for their employer for 26 weeks ending with the 15th week before the baby is due or the end of the week in which the child's adopter is notified of being matched with the child
- give the correct notice.

Employees should tell their employer as soon as possible that they wish to take paternity leave, but no later than the end of the 15th week before the expected week of childbirth. They should say when the baby is due, if they're going to take one or two weeks off, and when they expect their paternity leave to start. Those who are eligible can choose to take either one week or two consecutive weeks' paid paternity leave (not odd days).

Ordinary Paternity Pay

The employee must:

- be employed by the employer up to the date of birth
- earn at least the Lower Earnings Level a week (before tax) (see Appendix II).

Employees eligible for Statutory Paternity Pay are entitled to £138.18 per week or 90% of average weekly earning, if that is less (rate from April 2014). Employers may, however, give more and this may form part of the terms and conditions of employment.

Employees will need to take their paternity leave within 56 days of the actual date of birth of the child. Paternity leave cannot start until the birth of the baby; employees may be able to take some annual leave before.

There is no legal right to *paid* time off for antenatal appointments. However, it is open to employers to allow employees to take annual leave, or to swap shifts or make time up. These arrangements must be agreed with the employer in advance.

Shared Parental Leave

This new right will apply in respect of a baby due to be born on or after 5 April 2015, or for children who are placed for adoption on or after that date. After April 2015 Additional Paternity Leave and Pay will no longer be available.

Employee conditions

Additional Paternity Leave and Pay may be available if:

- the employee is the father of a child, partner or civil partner
- the employee and his partner receive notification that they are matched with a child for adoption
- the employee's wife, partner or civil partner is adopting a child from overseas and the child enters the UK
- the child's mother is entitled to Statutory Maternity Leave, Maternity Pay or Allowance, or Statutory Adoption Leave or Pay.

Additional Paternity Leave

This is for a maximum of 26 weeks. Leave can be taken any time from 20 weeks after the child is born, but it must have finished by the child's first birthday. In the case of adoption it can start any time between 20 weeks and 52 weeks after the child starts living with the adopter.

Notification conditions

To qualify for Additional Paternity Leave and Pay employers must be notified in writing at least eight weeks before the start of the leave. This must include:

- the expected date of the baby's birth or date of notification of being matched for adoption
- the actual date of baby's birth, or placement of adoption
- the start date of the Additional Paternity Leave and Pay
- relationship to the mother, and the leave being requested is to care for the child.

For Additional Paternity Leave and Pay to be taken, the child's mother or adopter must have started working again and any relevant payment must have stopped, with at least two weeks of the 39-week payment period remaining.

An employee must intend to care for the child during his Additional Statutory Paternity Pay period. Additional Statutory Paternity Pay is only payable during the period of the 39-week Maternity Allowance, Statutory Maternity or Statutory Adoption Pay period. It cannot continue beyond the end of the Statutory Maternity Pay, Maternity Allowance or Statutory Adoption Pay period.

The following flowcharts show the eligibility rules for both Ordinary Leave and Additional Leave and aims to simplify this complex issue.

Figure 6.1: **Ordinary Paternity Leave**

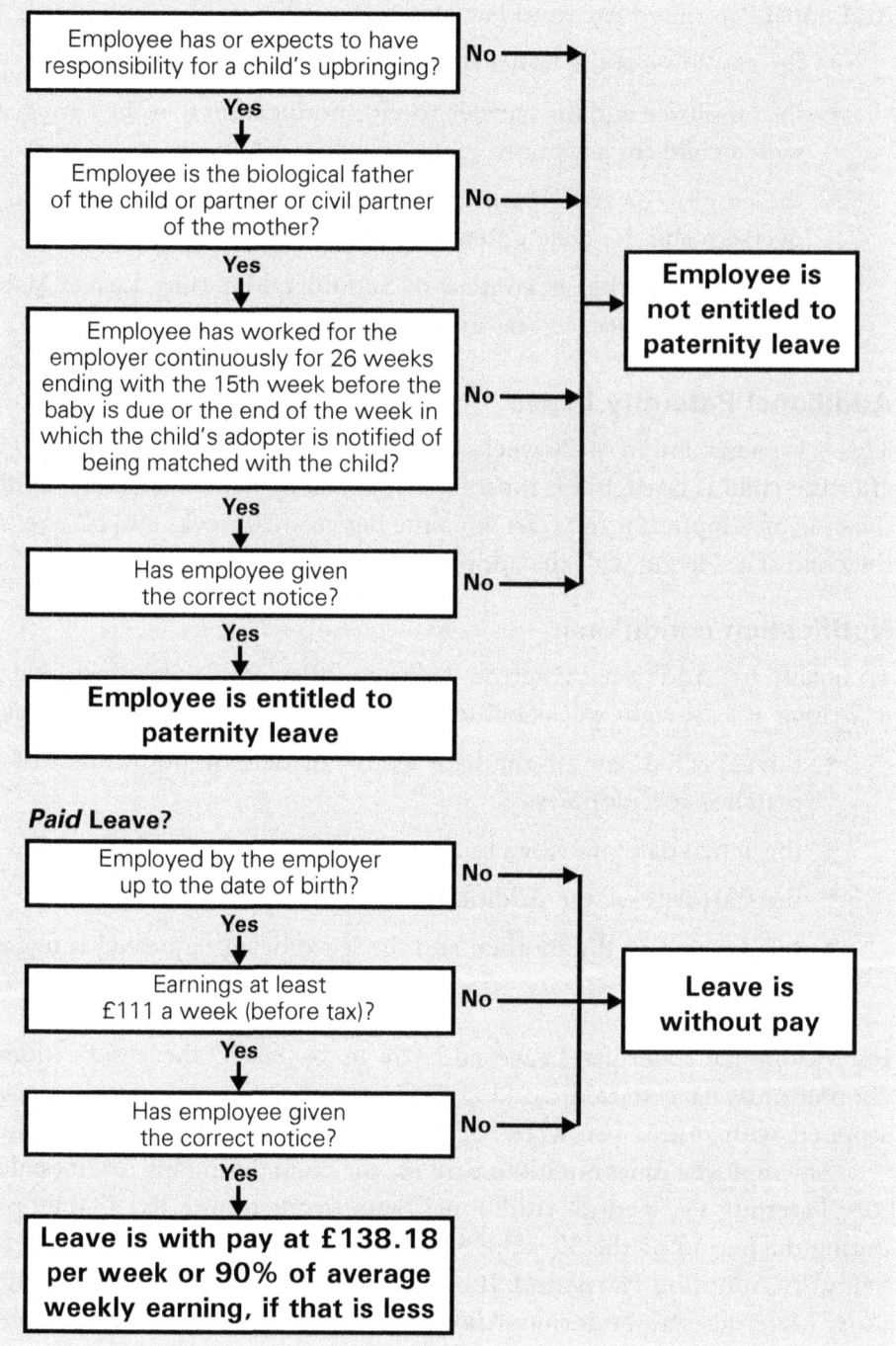

Figure 6.2: **Additional Paternity Leave**

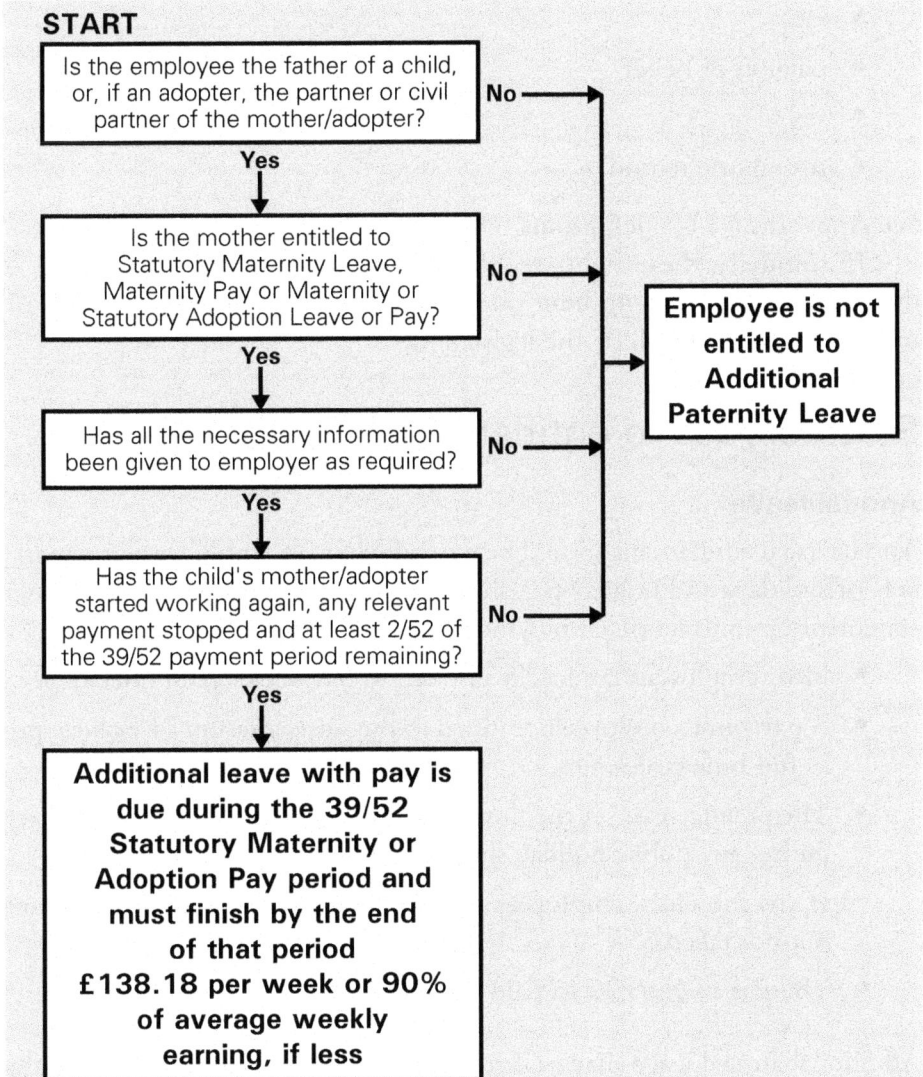

Equality rights

A full account of the equality legislation is set out in Appendix VI.
The nine protected characteristics are as follows:

- age
- disability
- gender reassignment
- marriage and civil partnership

- pregnancy and maternity
- race
- religion or belief
- sex
- sexual orientation.

See Appendix VI for definitions.

In summary, these rights require no qualifying service (unlike, say, unfair dismissal) and there is no limit on the compensation an employment tribunal may award for a breach of the legislation.

Statutory leave entitlement

Annual leave

Annual leave entitlement should be agreed when an employee starts work. Details of holidays and holiday pay should be set down in the employee's written statement or contract of employment.

- Most employees are legally entitled to 5.6 weeks' paid holiday per year.
- A part-time employee is entitled to the same amount of holiday pro rata as full-time colleagues.[7]
- The practice can set the times when employees can take their leave, e.g. during any public holiday shutdown.
- If the job ends, employees have the right to be paid for any leave due but not taken.
- There is *no legal right* to paid public holidays.

Additional annual leave may be agreed as part of the employment contract. A week of leave should allow employees to be away from work for a week, i.e. it should be the same amount of time as the working week. If an employee works a five-day week, he or she is entitled to 28 days' leave.

Part-timers are entitled to a proportion of 28 days based on the length of their working week. So, if they work a three-day week, their entitlement is 3/5 × 28 days, which equals 16.8 days' leave. The practice can set the times that employees take their statutory leave, e.g. for a public holiday shutdown. If someone's employment ends, he or she has a right to be paid for the leave due and not taken.

For an employee who works six days a week the statutory entitlement is capped at 28 days.

Carrying leave over from one leave year to the next

There is no automatic right to carry leave over to the next holiday year unless the employer agrees. This agreement may be written into the employment contract.

Public holidays

There is no legal right to paid leave for *public holidays*; any right to paid time off for these holidays depends on the terms of an employee's contract. Paid public holidays can be counted as part of the statutory 5.6 weeks of holiday.

Leave for dependants

An employee has a right to 'reasonable time off to deal with an emergency involving a dependant'.

A dependant could be a spouse, partner, child, grandchild, parent or someone who depends on the employee for care.

A 'reasonable' amount is defined as the necessary time to deal with the emergency. There is no set amount of time because it depends on the situation, and it is after all an emergency.

Limits on time off

Theoretically, there are no limits on how many times an employee can take time off for dependants. However, the practice may wish to talk to the employee if time off is affecting his or her work.

Pay

There is no requirement to pay an employee for time off to look after dependants. This will depend on the employment contract or possibly previous practice creating a precedent.

Summary of leave for dependants

- 'Reasonable' time off is given for emergencies involving the dependant.
- The dependant is a partner, child, parent, live-in relative or someone else reliant on the employee.
- Examples include dealing with illness or death, care arrangement problems, or incidents during school hours.
- The maximum is one or two days in most cases.
- No service is required and it may be unpaid.
- If the employee has advance knowledge, then holiday should be taken.

Parental leave

After one year's service a parent responsible for a child under five (18 if disabled) is entitled to take up to 18 weeks' leave *in total* for each eligible child, as follows.

Table 6.1: Entitlement for unpaid leave

Child	Entitlement
For each child	18 weeks up to their 5th birthday
For each adopted child	18 weeks up to their 18th birthday or 5th anniversary of their adoption, whichever comes first
For each child who qualifies for Disability Living Allowance	18 weeks up to their 18th birthday

Eligible employees can take unpaid parental leave to look after their child's welfare, e.g. to:

- spend more time with their children
- look at new schools
- settle children into new childcare arrangements
- spend more time with family, e.g. visiting grandparents.

Conditions

- Twenty-one days' notice is required.
- Taking four or more weeks' leave and returning to the old job may not be 'reasonably practicable'.
- A breach may lead to a complaint to a tribunal.
- The limit on the amount of leave a parent can take in a year is four weeks for each child (unless employer agrees otherwise).
- Parental leave is *unpaid* – unless an employment contract specifies otherwise.

An employee must take parental leave as whole weeks (e.g. one week or two weeks) rather than individual days, unless the practice agrees otherwise or if the child is disabled. The leave does not have to be taken all at once.

A 'week' equals the length of time an employee normally works over seven days.

Carrying parental leave over from a previous job

Parental leave applies to each child and not to an individual's job, so it can be carried over. A new employer may wish to seek confirmation of previous leave taken.

Flexible working

Flexible working is a way of working that suits an employee's needs, e.g. having flexible start and finish times, or working from home.

Flexible working rules are different in Northern Ireland.[8]

Changes to flexible working

From 30 June 2014 *all* employees have had the legal right to request flexible working – not just parents and carers. Employees must have worked for the same employer for at least 26 weeks to be eligible.

What employers must do

Employers must deal with requests in a 'reasonable manner'. Examples of handling requests in a reasonable manner include:

- assessing the advantages and disadvantages of the application
- holding a meeting to discuss the request with the employee
- offering an appeal process.

If an employer does not handle a request in a reasonable manner, the employee can take them to an employment tribunal.

An employer can refuse an application if they have a good business reason for doing so.

Types of flexible working

There are many different ways of working flexibly. The following are listed on the Gov.uk website.[9]

Job sharing

Two people do one job and split the hours.

Working from home

It might be possible to do some or all of the work from home or anywhere else other than the normal place of work.

Part time

An employee works less than full-time hours (usually by working fewer days).

Compressed hours

An employee works full-time hours but over fewer days.

Flexitime

The employee chooses when to start and finish work (within agreed limits) but works certain 'core hours', e.g. 10 a.m. to 4 p.m. every day.

Annualised hours

The employee has to work a certain number of hours over the year, but he or she has some flexibility about when he or she works such as school term times. There are sometimes 'core hours' that the employee regularly works each week, and the employee works the rest of his or her hours flexibly or when there is extra demand at work.

Staggered hours

The employee has different start, finish and break times from other workers.

Phased retirement

Since the default retirement age has been phased out older workers can now choose when they want to retire. This means they can reduce their hours and work part time if the employer agrees.

Applying for flexible working

Employees can apply for flexible working if they have worked continuously for the same employer for the last 26 weeks. This is known as 'making a statutory application'.

The basic steps are:

- the employee writes to the employer
- the employer considers the request and makes a decision within three months – or longer if agreed with the employee
- the employer may agree to the request. If so they must change the terms and conditions in the employment contract
- the employer may disagree, in which case they must write to the employee giving the business reasons for the refusal. The employee may be able to complain to an employment tribunal.

Employees can only apply once for flexible working in any 12-month period.

Writing to the employer

An employee should email or write a letter to his or her employer. Employers may ask employees to use a standard form to make an application.[10]

The application must include:

- the date
- a statement that this is a statutory request
- details of how the employee wants to work flexibly and when he or she wants to start
- an explanation of how the employee thinks flexible working might affect the business and how this could be dealt with, e.g. if he or she is not at work on certain days
- a statement saying if and when the employee has made a previous application.

Withdrawing an application

Employees should tell their employer in writing if they want to withdraw their application.

The employer can treat an application as withdrawn if the employee misses two meetings to discuss an application or appeal without good reason, e.g. sickness. In this case the employer must tell the employee they are treating the request as withdrawn.

Remember, practices must consider flexible working requests in a 'reasonable manner'. An employer should usually make a decision within three months of the request (longer only if agreed with the employee).

If agreeing the application

The employer should write to the employee with:

- a statement of the agreed changes
- a start date for flexible working.

They should also change the employee's contract to include the new terms and conditions.[11]

This should be done as soon as possible but no later than 28 days after the request was approved.

If rejecting an application

The employer must tell the employee that they have rejected the application.

Reasons for rejecting

Employers can reject an application for any of the following reasons:

- extra costs that will damage the business

- the work cannot be reorganised among other staff
- people cannot be recruited to do the work
- flexible working will affect quality and performance
- the business will not be able to meet customer demand
- there is a lack of work to do during the proposed working times
- the practice is planning changes to the workforce.

Appeals

Employees no longer have a statutory right to an appeal. But offering an appeals process helps to demonstrate that the employer is handling requests in a 'reasonable manner'.

How to appeal

The employee must follow the practice's procedures for appealing. The employee or employer should follow the practice's grievance procedure if a rejected application causes problems.[12]

Employment tribunal complaint

Employees can complain to an employment tribunal if the employer:

- did not handle the request in a 'reasonable manner'
- wrongly treated the employee's application as withdrawn
- dismissed or treated an employee poorly because of his or her flexible working request, e.g. refused a promotion or pay rise
- rejected an application based on incorrect facts.

Employees cannot complain to a tribunal just because their flexible working request was rejected.

An employee has to complain to the tribunal within three months of:

- hearing his or her employer's decision
- hearing his or her request was treated as withdrawn
- the date the employer should have responded to his or her request (but failed to do so).

Useful information

Some useful documents include Acas's *Handling in a Reasonable Manner Requests to Work Flexibly*[13] and Gov.uk's specimen application form.[10]

Part-time employees

Part-timers are protected. They cannot be treated less favourably than equivalent full-timers just because they are part time.

To state the obvious, a part-time employee is someone who works fewer hours than a full-time employee. However, there is no specific number of hours in law that make someone full or part time, but a full-time employee will usually work 35 hours or more a week.

Part-time employees should get the same treatment for:

- pay rates (including sick pay, maternity, paternity and adoption leave and pay)
- pension opportunities and benefits
- holidays
- training and career development
- selection for promotion and transfer, or for redundancy
- opportunities for career breaks.

Some benefits are applied pro rata (in proportion to hours worked). For example, if full-timers get a £1000 Christmas bonus, and a part-timer works half the number of hours, the part-timer should get £500.

Overtime pay

Part-timers may not get overtime pay until they have worked over the normal hours of a full-timer.

When employers can treat part-time employees differently

There are some situations when employers do not have to treat part-timers in the same way as full-time employees. In these situations the employer must be able to show there is a good reason to do so – the 'objective justification'.

Example

An employer may provide health insurance for full-time employees but not part-timers if this can be objectively justified. Their reason may be that the costs involved are disproportionate to the benefits part-timers are entitled to. In this case the employer may come up with an alternative like asking the part-time worker to make a contribution to the extra cost.

If a part-timer has been treated less favourably

Part-timers have the right to get a written statement of reasons for the treatment from their employer. The request should be in writing and the employer must write back within 21 days.

If the employee is not satisfied that the reason given was objectively justified, he or she may be able to take a case to an employment tribunal.

Temporary contracts

A fixed-term contract (FTC) is one that will terminate at a future date when a specific 'term' expires – the completion of a particular project or task, the occurrence or non-occurrence of a specific event.

An employee may be fixed term if he or she is: a seasonal or casual employee taken on for up to six months during a peak period; a specialist employee for a project; or covering for maternity leave.

An FTC should state the date the contract is expected to end and the reason it is for a fixed-term period. FTCs are covered by legislation – the Fixed-Term Employees (Prevention of Less Favourable Treatment) Regulations 2002.[14] These regulations are designed to prevent less favourable treatment of temps in comparison with their permanent colleagues.

Temps are entitled to the same terms and conditions of employment as other employees concerning, for example, perks, holiday entitlements, training, in redundancy situations, in promotion situations, pension schemes and access to permanent job vacancies. A 'comparable' permanent employee is someone who works for the same employer, doing the same or a similar job.

However, employers can justify giving temps less favourable treatment than permanent employees for certain, genuine business reasons.

The regulations also prevent the successive use of FTCs, where a permanent contract should be given.

Exemptions

These regulations do not apply to apprentices and do not apply to *workers* (e.g. casual staff, agency temps) or freelancers/contractors and agency workers.

An employer is under no legal obligation to *offer* a post-holder on an FTC the same job if it is made permanent. What the employer must do is to give him or her *access to apply* for permanent vacancies though (unless this lack of access can be objectively justified).

Four years' employment

Where an employee has been continuously employed on successive FTCs for four years or more he or she should automatically receive permanent status, unless the employer has an objective reason (at the point the contract was last renewed) for not offering a permanent contract that justifies a renewal for a further fixed-term period.

An employee with four years' continuous service can ask the employer for a written statement confirming that he or she is now a permanent employee and is no longer employed on an FTC.

If the employer fails to give this statement (when it has been requested) or gives a statement of reasons why an employee must remain on an FTC that the employee does not agree with, he or she can state a grievance and possibly make a claim to an employment tribunal.

What happens when FTCs expire?

Although it may seem strange, the expiry of an FTC is a *dismissal in law* and FTC holders with two years' service have a right not to be unfairly dismissed. Employers must therefore follow a fair procedure to ensure that there is a fair dismissal (see Chapter 5).

In many cases the reason for dismissal will be redundancy (as the requirement for the employee to do the work has ceased or diminished and there is a reduction in the number of employees). Therefore the employer must follow a fair redundancy procedure, which includes:

- an obligation to consult with the employee about the forthcoming expiry of his or her contract and to consider alternative employment/redeployment
- the selection for redundancy must be fair and not made purely on the basis of the employee's FTC status – there must be an objective reason for the redundancy.

With two years' continuous service, the temp will be entitled to a statutory redundancy payment.

Other reasons to legitimately end an FTC are capability, conduct or some other substantial reason (SOSR). SOSR is often used if the FTC was given to cover for maternity or sick leave and the permanent employee returns so the person on the FTC is no longer needed. However, appropriate procedures still need to be followed including consultation with the individual and looking for alternative jobs within the practice.

Notice periods

The employer does *not* have to give notice that the contract is ending on its expected date, although the employer may do this. However, if notice for an early termination is written into the contract the employer may be able to terminate the contract *before* its nominated end date by giving the appropriate notice.

This must be at least the statutory minimum notice period applicable to the employee's service.

If there is no notice period and the contract does not allow for early termination but the contract is ended early, this may be a breach of contract (except where the employee has committed gross misconduct). Then there may be a claim for compensation at an employment tribunal for the earnings during the remainder of the contract term.

To confirm, in both situations the employee can only claim for unfair dismissal and/or redundancy pay if he or she has two years' continuous service.

The employee cannot claim for breach of contract if the contract expires on its proper end date or he or she is given notice that the contract will end early and given the correct notice period, as set out in the written contract.

Whatever the reason for ending the contract early, the employer must follow the appropriate dismissal or redundancy procedures. See again Chapter 5.

If the FTC ends on its expiry date and it is not renewed, or notice given to end it early, with two years' continuous service the employee is entitled to ask for a written statement from the employer explaining the reasons why the contract is ending.

How to end an FTC reasonably

An FTC normally ends automatically at its completion date and there is no need for the employer to give notice. However, the decision not to renew a contract is still a *form of dismissal* and the employer must still act fairly, otherwise a claim may arise for unfair dismissal. The employee has the right to:

- not be unfairly dismissed (following two years' service)
- a written statement of reasons for the dismissal (after one year's service)
- statutory redundancy pay (after two years' service).

Bearing this in mind, the following procedure is suggested.

1. *Assemble the facts concerning the FTC.* This covers the date of commencement, the expected date of termination and the length of service the FTC holder will have at termination.

2. *Inform the FTC holder that a meeting is required.* Explain in writing that you wish to discuss the impending end of his or her FTC.

3. *Hold a meeting with the FTC holder to discuss matters – not necessarily the same day.* At the meeting the employer should explain that the ending of the FTC is a 'technical' dismissal and would the contract holder want to discuss any possible alternatives? (The individual may have other plans anyway.) The employer may explain that there is in effect a redundancy

– with no alternative job available. If so obtain the FTC holder's views.

4. *Allow the employee to be accompanied at the meeting by a colleague or union official.* Employees have a statutory right to be accompanied by a companion. The chosen companion may be a fellow worker, a trade union representative or an official employed by a trade union.

5. *Decide on appropriate action.* After the meeting decide what to do, offer an alternative job or notify the FTC holder that he or she is effectively redundant with no alternative on offer to the contract ending. If he or she has two years' service then redundancy pay is in order (see Chapter 5).

6. *Provide employees with an opportunity to appeal.* Arrange for one of the partners to hear the appeal and discuss his or her decision at a partners' meeting (and take minutes). Notify the FTC holder of the final decision.

Health and safety

This section is taken from the Health and Safety Executive (HSE) website.[15]

Employers' responsibilities

Under the law employers are responsible for health and safety management. The following provides a broad outline of how the law applies to employers. Do not forget: employees and the self-employed have important responsibilities too.[16]

It is an employer's duty to protect the health, safety and welfare of employees and other people who might be affected by their business. Employers must do whatever is reasonably practicable to achieve this.

This means making sure that employees and others are protected from anything that may cause harm, effectively controlling any risks to injury or health that could arise in the workplace.

Employers' duties under health and safety law

- To assess risks in the workplace. Risk assessments should be carried out that address all risks that might cause harm in the workplace.

- Employers must give information to employees about the risks in the workplace and how employees are protected, also instruct and train them on how to deal with the risks.

- Employers must consult employees on health and safety issues. Consultation must be either direct or through a safety representative that is elected by the workforce.

For more details on the basics of what employers must do to make their business comply with health and safety law in a low-risk business, HSE has produced a guide, *Health and Safety Made Simple*.[17]

Another HSE publication, *Health and Safety Regulation: a short guide*, has more details on how health and safety law is meant to work.[18]

Employers have a legal duty under the Health and Safety Information for Employees Regulations (HSIER) to display the approved poster in a prominent position in each workplace[19] or to provide each employee with a copy of the approved leaflet 'Health and safety law: what you need to know', which outlines British health and safety law.[20]

If employees think their employer is exposing them to risks or is not carrying out their legal duties with regards to health and safety, and if this has been pointed out to them but no satisfactory response has been received, employees can make a complaint to HSE.[21]

Employment scenarios

1. Full-time staff are entitled to have bank holidays off. A part-time member of staff who does not work on Mondays wants time off in lieu for bank holiday Monday.

    What is the legal position?

2. Your practice nurse mentions that her young daughter's child minder is (not for the first time) going to be unavailable, this time next Monday. The nurse would be working that day so she asks for the day off.

    How do you respond to this?

References

1. Employment status. www.gov.uk/employment-status/employee [accessed 13 November 2014].
2. Acas. Shared parental leave and pay. www.acas.org.uk/index.aspx?articleid=4911 [accessed 13 November 2014].
3. Shared Parental Leave and Pay: employer guide. www.gov.uk/shared-parental-leave-and-pay-employer-guide [accessed 20 November 2014].
4. Calculate your maternity pay or benefits. www.gov.uk/calculate-your-maternity-pay [accessed 13 November 2014].
5. Maternity allowance. www.gov.uk/maternity-allowance/overview [accessed 13 November 2014].
6. Sure Start Maternity Grant. www.gov.uk/sure-start-maternity-grant/how-to-claim [accessed 13 November 2014].

7. Holiday entitlement. www.gov.uk/holiday-entitlement-rights/holiday-pay-the-basics [accessed 13 November 2014].
8. NIdirect Government Services. Flexible working. www.nidirect.gov.uk/flexible-working [accessed 13 November 2014].
9. Flexible working. www.gov.uk/flexible-working/overview [accessed 13 November 2014].
10. Right to request flexible working: application form. www.gov.uk/government/publications/the-right-to-request-flexible-working-form [accessed 13 November 2014].
11. Changing an employment contract. www.gov.uk/your-employment-contract-how-it-can-be-changed [accessed 13 November 2014].
12. Solve a workplace dispute. www.gov.uk/solve-workplace-dispute [accessed 13 November 2014].
13. Acas. *Handling in a Reasonable Manner Requests to Work Flexibly*. Norwich: TSO, 2014. www.acas.org.uk/media/pdf/f/e/Code-of-Practice-on-handling-in-a-reasonable-manner-requests-to-work-flexibly.pdf [accessed 13 November 2014].
14. The Fixed-Term Employees (Prevention of Less Favourable Treatment) Regulations 2002. www.legislation.gov.uk/uksi/2002/2034/contents/made.
15. Health and Safety Executive. Employer's responsibilities. www.hse.gov.uk/workers/employers.htm [accessed 13 November 2014].
16. Health and Safety Executive. Are you an employee. www.hse.gov.uk/workers/responsibilities.htm [accessed 13 November 2014].
17. Health and Safety Executive. *Health and Safety Made Simple: the basics for your business*. London: HSE, 2014. www.hse.gov.uk/simple-health-safety/index.htm [accessed 13 November 2014].
18. Health and Safety Executive. *Health and Safety Regulation: a short guide*. London: HSE, n.d. www.hse.gov.uk/pubns/hsc13.pdf [accessed 13 November 2014].
19. Health and safety law poster – frequently asked questions (FAQ). www.hse.gov.uk/contact/faqs/lawposter.htm [accessed 13 November 2014].
20. Health and safety law (leaflet). www.hse.gov.uk/pubns/books/lawleaflet.htm [accessed 13 November 2014].
21. Health and Safety Executive. Complaints. www.hse.gov.uk/contact/complaints.htm [accessed 13 November 2014].

7

Other issues

Staff appraisal
Workplace stress
Example of a stress policy
Grievance procedures
Transfer of Undertakings – TUPE

Staff appraisal

General principles

- Appraisals can benefit both employers and employees by improving job performance, by making it easier to identify strengths and weaknesses, and by determining suitability for development.

- In designing a scheme it is necessary to decide who should be appraised, who does the appraising, how often appraisals take place and whether employees should see their appraisal reports.

- Employers are not required by law to introduce appraisal schemes. There are however some aspects of employment legislation that affect appraisal.

Objectives

The main objectives of an appraisal system are usually to review performance, potential and identify training and career planning needs. In addition the appraisal system may be used to determine whether employees should receive an element of financial reward for their performance.

Benefits

Appraisals can help to improve employees' job performance by identifying strengths and weaknesses, and determining how their strengths can be best utilised within the organisation and weaknesses overcome. They can help to reveal problems that may be restricting employees' progress and causing inefficient work practices.

An appraisal system can develop a greater degree of consistency by ensuring that managers and employees meet formally and regularly to discuss performance and potential. Experience shows this can encourage better performance from employees.

A formal appraisal system?

It is important that the appraisal system is designed to meet the particular needs of the practice and is not over-complicated. An appraisal system does not need to generate a lot of paper to be effective; on the contrary, the most effective systems are often the simplest.

No practice, whether large or small, should contemplate the introduction of a formal appraisal system unless it is fully committed to its success and clear about its objectives. A scheme will involve the investment of time and money. On the other hand, a badly designed appraisal system operated by untrained and poorly motivated managers, and hastily introduced, will damage relationships and provide no benefits.

Who carries out the appraisal?

Generally, employees are appraised by their immediate managers, since those who delegate work and monitor performance are best placed to appraise performance. Others argue that appraisals carried out by a higher level allow employees an opportunity to talk with higher management, who can find out the views and attitudes of more junior staff at first hand.

A better approach may be for employees' immediate superiors to carry out appraisals and for partners to have an opportunity to comment on the report. This enables partners to keep a regular check on the progress of staff and to monitor the appraisal system to ensure that reporting standards are consistent.

Frequency

Employee appraisal should be a continuous process and should not be limited to a formal review once a year. In a high-technology organisation objectives may be changing quickly so that formal appraisals may need to be carried out more than once a year. Most employees receive a formal appraisal annually, although more frequent appraisals are often needed for new employees, for longer serving staff who have moved to new posts or for those who are below acceptable performance standards.

Transparency of reports

It is sometimes argued that 'open reporting' discourages managers from giving candid appraisals of staff. In order to avoid conflict managers may not accurately convey some of the more critical comments they have written on the report. However, if employees are unable to see their reports they will not know whether the verbal feedback accurately reflects what was put on the report by the manager or the areas where improvement is required.

In practice, managers are more likely to make fair and accurate comments on the appraisal form if they are aware that the form will be shown to the employee and that they will have to substantiate their written comments at the appraisal interview. If managers have a tendency to be too generous in an open reporting system, this can be counteracted by training, monitoring and by allowing more partners to comment on the reports.

Legal issues

There is no legal obligation on employers to introduce appraisal systems. However, some employment legislation does affect employee appraisal.

The Data Protection Act

This covers computer records and some manual records kept in structured form, and are thus likely to cover most appraisal records. The general principles of the act are that employees should have access to personal information and expect that the confidentiality of this information is respected by the employer.

Equality provisions

Employees who feel that they have been refused promotion or access to training on grounds of their race, sex, age or disability, or any of the other 'protected characteristics' set out in the Equality Act 2010 (or the alternative legislation in Northern Ireland), have the right to make a complaint to an employment tribunal. In addition, in Northern Ireland discrimination based on political opinion is unlawful.

Employees dismissed on grounds of inadequate performance

Appraisal schemes should not be used as a disciplinary mechanism to deal with poor performers but it is important to establish a procedure for informing employees in writing of unsatisfactory assessments. The consequences of failure to meet the required standards should be explained to the employee and confirmed in writing.

Design

It is essential to have written records of the appraisal to provide feedback to employees and to allow partners to monitor the effectiveness of appraisals. The job description helps to focus attention on the employee's performance at work and to avoid assessing character.

Some appraisal techniques are as follows:

- *rating* – a number of employee characteristics are rated on a scale that may range from 'outstanding' to 'unacceptable'
- *comparison with objectives* – employees and their managers agree objectives. The appraisal is based on how far these objectives have been met
- *critical incidents* – the appraiser records incidents of employees' positive and negative behaviour during a given period
- *narrative report* – the appraiser describes the individual's work performance in his or her own words.

Making a success of appraisals

- Ensure that partners are fully committed to the idea of appraisals.
- Consult with senior staff and employees about the design and implementation of appraisals before they are introduced.
- Monitor schemes regularly.
- Give appraisers training to enable them to make fair and objective assessments and to carry out effective appraisal interviews.
- Keep the scheme as simple and straightforward as possible.

A checklist

The partners must be committed to the idea of appraisals. They should fully accept that those who carry out the appraisals will need to be properly trained and have sufficient time and resources available to complete interviews, fill in the forms and carry out follow-up work.

Consult with employees before appraisals are introduced. Agreement should be sought about the objectives and the appraisal methods.

Make the scheme as straightforward as possible. Appraisal systems can sometimes fail because of over-elaborate paper work. It is essential to design the recording systems for those who will be using them and to keep any forms as simple and as clearly written as possible.

A timetable should be fixed for the implementation of the scheme.

Provide adequate training. All managers who carry out appraisals must receive training to help them assess performance effectively and to put that skill into use in the appraisal process. Appraisers should receive written instructions on how to complete reports and they should also be given the opportunity to practise these skills and to receive feedback on their performance.

Make sure that managers carry out appraisals. Some appraisal schemes fail simply because managers give low priority to appraisals. A partner should therefore be given responsibility for coordinating the scheme and for ensuring that interviews are held and that the forms are completed correctly. The appraisal of a manager's own performance can usefully include consideration of how effectively he or she undertakes appraisals.

Some organisations set an annual timetable for the completion of various stages of the appraisal process and circulate this timetable to all appraisers. Another method is to spread appraisals throughout the year, possibly on the anniversary of the employee's appointment. This takes the pressure off the manager to carry out a large number of appraisals at the same time.

Monitor the appraisal system. Check that appraisals are being carried out properly and determine whether the system needs to be modified to meet the changing needs of the organisation. The views of supervisors should be obtained about the scheme in general and in relation to any problems they have encountered. It is also important to get reactions from employees. The appraisal system should be updated regularly. Schemes will become ineffective if they are not modified to take account of changes in the practice, in services, skills and jobs, or arising from the introduction of new technology.

Workplace stress

Stress is the adverse reaction people have to excessive pressure. It is not a disease. However, if stress is intense and goes on for some time, it can lead to mental and physical ill health (e.g. depression, nervous breakdown, heart disease).

Pressure is part and parcel of all work and helps to keep everyone motivated. But excessive pressure can lead to stress, which undermines performance, is costly to employers and can make people ill. To quote Acas, research has shown that:

- 12.8 million working days were lost to stress, depression and anxiety in 2004/5
- each new case of stress leads to an average of 29 days off work
- work-related stress is widespread, and up to 5 million people in the UK feel 'very' or 'extremely' stressed by their work

- work-related stress costs society about £3.7 billion every year
- young people experience the worst workplace stress because they feel less able to raise the issue
- people tend to hide stress as something you should not 'bring to work'
- people worry about 'stress' going on their personnel records, that it will be seen as a weakness.

Clearly work-related stress is a serious problem in some organisations. Tackling it effectively can result in significant benefits. There are practical things managers can do to prevent and control work-related stress. Moreover, it is an employer's duty in law to make sure that employees are not made ill by work-related stress.

The costs of stress may show up as:

- high staff turnover
- an increase in sickness absence
- reduced work performance
- poor timekeeping
- more patient complaints.

Stress in one person can also lead to stress in staff who have to cover for their colleague. Also, employers who do not take stress seriously may leave themselves open to compensation claims from employees who have suffered ill health from work-related stress. According to BUPA, signs of stress may be seen (see Table 7.1).

It is likely that many people suffer from a couple of these symptoms some of the time – we all do. However, if these symptoms are shown most of the time, then this is indicative of a current stress-related problem.

Where there are concerns about stress, a practice should review the work to check whether it carries a risk of stress-related injury. There should be a risk assessment as part of the health and safety policy, or even a stress audit among staff. The audit can be done by using questionnaires or by talking to staff, individually or in groups.

A risk of stress-related injury may be apparent from the volume or stressful nature of the work. Practices should take note of any warning signs in staff, e.g. higher than usual sickness absences.

Where an employee actually tells the employer that he or she cannot cope, it may be hard for the employer to evade liability for any subsequent breakdown unless reasonable steps had been taken to reduce the burden on the employee. Such steps might include establishing a stress management programme (see Table 7.2, overleaf).

To protect themselves from possible legal action, practices are advised to have in place a stress management policy to avoid the risk of damages being sought against them by their employees.

Practices should take the following steps:

- investigate stress levels and their likely causes
- seek Occupational Health advice for individuals
- make sure individuals are well matched to their jobs
- set clearly defined objectives for staff
- provide training in interpersonal skills
- have proper procedures for investigating complaints (from staff)
- consider flexible working hours
- provide opportunities for staff to contribute ideas – at regular consultative meetings
- provide support for staff experiencing high stress levels.

Table 7.1: **Behavioural and physical signs of stress**

Behavioural signs	*Physical signs*
Constant irritability with other people	Lack of appetite
Difficulty in making decisions	Craving for food when under pressure
Loss of sense of humour	Frequent indigestion or heartburn
Suppressed anger	Constipation or diarrhoea
Difficulty concentrating	Insomnia
Inability to finish one task before starting another	Tendency to sweat for no good reason
Feeling the target of other people's animosity	Nervous twitches, nail biting, etc.
Feeling unable to cope, tiredness	Headaches, cramps, muscle spasms, nausea
Lack of interest in doing things after work	Eczema

Source: Bupa. Stress.[1]

Table 7.2: **Stress management programme**

Main causes of stress	*What you can do about it*
Demands: employees often become overloaded if they cannot cope with the amount of work or type of work they are asked to do	Pay attention to the way the job is designed, training needs and whether it is possible for employees to work more flexible hours
Control: employees can feel disaffected and perform poorly if they have no say over how and when they do their work	Think about how employees are actively involved in decision making, the contribution made by teams and how reviewing performance can help identify strengths and weaknesses
Support: levels of sickness absence often rise if employees feel they cannot talk to managers about issues that are troubling them	Give employees the opportunity to talk about the issues causing stress, provide a sympathetic ear and keep them informed
Relationships: a failure to build relationships based on good behaviour and trust can lead to problems related to discipline, grievances and bullying	Check the organisation's policies for handling grievances, unsatisfactory performance, poor attendance and misconduct, and for tackling bullying and harassment
Role: employees will feel anxious about their work and the organisation if they don't know what is expected of them	Review the induction process, work out an accurate job description and maintain a close link between individual targets and organisational goals
Change: change needs to be managed effectively or it can lead to huge uncertainty and insecurity	Plan ahead so change doesn't come out of the blue. Consult with employees so they have a real input, and work together to solve problems

Example of a stress policy

(Print on practice headed paper)

Introduction
We are committed to protecting the health, safety and welfare of our staff and we recognise that workplace stress is a health and safety issue, and we acknowledge the importance of identifying and reducing workplace stressors. This policy will apply to everyone in the practice and [*the practice manager*] is responsible for implementation, with the practice responsible for providing the necessary resources.

Definition of stress
The Health and Safety Executive defines stress as 'the adverse reaction people have to excessive pressure or other types of demand placed on them'. This

makes an important distinction between pressure, which can be a positive state if managed correctly, and stress, which can be detrimental to health.

Policy
- The practice will identify all workplace stressors and conduct risk assessments to eliminate stress or control the risks from stress. These risk assessments will be regularly reviewed.
- The practice will consult with staff on all proposed action relating to the prevention of workplace stress.
- The practice will provide training for all partners and supervisory staff in good management practices.
- The practice will provide confidential counselling for staff affected by stress caused by either work or external factors.
- The practice will provide adequate resources to enable managers to implement the practice's agreed stress management strategy.

Responsibilities – practice manager and partners
- Conduct and implement recommendations of risk assessments.
- Ensure good communication between management and staff, particularly where there are organisational and procedural changes.
- Ensure staff are fully trained to discharge their duties.
- Ensure staff are provided with meaningful developmental opportunities.
- Monitor workloads to ensure that people are not overloaded.
- Monitor working hours and overtime to ensure that staff are not overworking. Monitor holidays to ensure that staff are taking their full entitlement.
- Monitor the effectiveness of measures to address stress by collating sickness absence statistics.
- Attend training as requested in good management practice and health and safety.
- Ensure that bullying and harassment are not tolerated within the practice.
- Be vigilant and offer additional support to a member of staff who is experiencing stress outside work, e.g. bereavement or separation.
- Support individuals who have been off sick with stress and advise them and their management on a planned return to work.

Responsibilities – employees
- Raise issues of concern with your practice manager, supervisor or Occupational Health if necessary.
- Accept opportunities for counselling when recommended.

Signed on behalf of the partners:
Staff Partner:
Date:

Grievance procedures

Ensuring that people are treated fairly and reducing conflict are important factors in the creation of a productive working environment. Employers and employees should seek informally to resolve most matters that arise in the course of the working relationship. This helps minor concerns to be resolved speedily without the need to have recourse to formal action. It also limits disruption to work and reduces any personal embarrassment in discussing issues of concern.

However, grievance procedures are essential when informal mechanisms are ineffective, or where they are inappropriate given the nature of the issue arising. These procedures can also help prevent unnecessary staff turnover and absenteeism, as well as avoiding costly and time-consuming tribunal cases.

It is essential that those implementing these procedures have the necessary training and guidance to do so, in line not just with minimum legal obligations but also with the principles of fairness and natural justice reflected in the Acas Code.

The Acas Code

This statutory code provides basic practical guidance on discipline and grievance handling in the workplace. It came into effect in 2009. Unlike the earlier code, it does not require employers and employees to follow mandatory steps in the process.

Employment tribunals will use the code when considering relevant cases, taking into account factors such as the size and resources of a business. If a tribunal regards a failure by either the employee or the employer to follow the code as unreasonable, it will have the power to adjust awards up or down by up to 25%.

The full Acas Code and guidance is available online.[2]

Keys steps in handling grievances in the workplace

1. *Employee notifies the employer about the nature of the grievance*

    If it is not possible to resolve a grievance informally employees should raise the matter formally, and without unreasonable delay, with a manager who is not the subject of the grievance. This should be done *in writing* and should set out the nature of the grievance.

2. *Hold a meeting with the employee to discuss the grievance*

    Employers should arrange for a formal meeting to be held without unreasonable delay after a written grievance is received.

    Employers, employees and their representatives should make every effort to attend the meeting. Employees should be allowed to explain their grievance and how they think it should be resolved. Consideration should be given to adjourning the meeting for any investigation that may be necessary.

3. *Allow the employee to be accompanied at the meeting*

    Employees have a statutory right to be accompanied by a representative at a grievance meeting that deals with a complaint about a duty owed by the employer to the employee. This applies where the complaint is, for example, that the employer is not honouring the employee's contract, or is in breach of legislation.

    The chosen representative may be a fellow employee, a trade union representative or a trade union official.

    The representative should be allowed to address the hearing, to put and sum up the employee's case, respond on behalf of the employee to any views expressed at the meeting and confer with the employee during the hearing. The representative does not, however, have the right to answer questions on the employee's behalf, address the hearing if the employee does not wish it or prevent the employer from explaining his or her case.

4. *Decide on appropriate action*

    Following the meeting decide on what action, if any, to take. Decisions should be communicated to the employee *in writing* without unreasonable delay and, where appropriate, should set out what action the employer intends to take to resolve the grievance. The employee should be informed that he or she can appeal if not content with the action taken.

5. *Allow the employee to take the grievance further if not resolved*

    Where an employee feels that his or her grievance has not been satisfactorily resolved, the employee can appeal. He or she should let the employer know the grounds for his or her appeal without unreasonable delay and *in writing*.

    - Appeals should be heard without unreasonable delay and at a time and place that should be notified to the employee in advance.
    - The appeal should be dealt with impartially and wherever possible by a manager who has not previously been involved in the case.
    - Employees have a statutory right to be accompanied at any such appeal hearing.
    - The outcome of the appeal should be communicated to the employee in writing without unreasonable delay.

6. *Overlapping grievance and disciplinary cases*

    Where an employee raises a grievance during a disciplinary process the disciplinary process may be temporarily suspended in order to deal with the grievance. Where the grievance and disciplinary cases are related it may be appropriate to deal with both issues concurrently.

Transfer of Undertakings – TUPE

What is TUPE?

TUPE refers to the Transfer of Undertakings (Protection of Employment) Regulations 2006, as amended by the Collective Redundancies and Transfer of Undertakings (Protection of Employment) (Amendment) Regulations 2014.

The TUPE rules apply to organisations of all sizes and protect employees' rights when the organisation *or service* they work for *transfers to a new employer*. There are impacts for the transferor (the outgoing employer) and the transferee (the incoming employer) as well as for the employees concerned.

TUPE would apply if a GP practice takes on a contract for a list of patients formerly looked after by another practice. The transferor may be a single-handed GP who is retiring and has no immediate successor. The transfer may pass through the hands of the Primary Care Trust or Health Board, or it may go directly to the ultimate transferee. In both situations TUPE applies.

How TUPE impacts in practice

Employees from the newly acquired business or contract will transfer automatically to the incoming employer. Their terms and conditions of employment and continuity of service are preserved and transfer at the same time, and they also receive certain protections around dismissal and redundancy. This means they take their length of service with them as if they had always worked for the incoming employer.

Practices should take the TUPE rules into account when deciding how to bid for a contract and allow for the timetables involved in a transfer due to legal requirements such as consultation periods.

When TUPE applies

There are two situations when the TUPE regulations may apply: business transfers and service provision transfers.

Business transfers

The TUPE regulations apply if a business or part of a business moves to a new owner or merges with another business to make a brand new employer. A part of a business might for example be the district midwifery function provided by a local trust.

Service provision transfers

The TUPE regulations apply in the following situations:

- a contractor takes over activities from a client (known as outsourcing)
- a new contractor takes over activities from another contractor (known as re-tendering)
- a client takes over activities from a contractor (known as insourcing).

Terms and conditions under TUPE

Following a transfer, employers often find they have employees with different terms and conditions working alongside each other and wish to change and harmonise terms and conditions. However, TUPE protects against change and harmonisation *for an indefinite period* if the sole or principal reason for the change is the transfer. Any such changes will be void.

Employers seeking to change terms that are unrelated to a transfer should seek legal advice to ensure this is the case and also read the Acas advice.[3]

Disclosure of Employee Liability Information

The outgoing employer must provide information about transferring employees to the incoming employer, and this is called Employee Liability Information. Among other things this includes the identity of the employees who will transfer, their contractual terms, and disciplinary and grievance history.

The information must be accurate, up to date and secure, and provided not less than 14 days before the transfer.

Information and consultation

Employers must inform/consult with employees through 'appropriate' elected representatives who could be formally elected employee representatives. In the absence of recognised trade unions or staff representatives, employers must arrange elections amongst the affected employees to elect representatives to consult about the transfer.

Dismissal and redundancies

Employers are often able to minimise or prevent redundancies and other dismissals when transfers take place. However, there will be occasions when they cannot be avoided. If an employee is dismissed either before or after a transfer and the sole or principal reason for the dismissal is the transfer, it will be automatically unfair.

Employees who believe that their terms and conditions have been substantially changed to their detriment before or after a transfer have the right to terminate their employment and claim *constructive unfair dismissal* at a tribunal. TUPE classifies these types of resignations as dismissals.

If as a result of a transfer a potential redundancy situation arises, there is a legal requirement to consult with employees individually.

For more information about redundancy generally see Chapter 5.

References

1. Bupa. Stress. www.bupa.co.uk/health-information/directory/s/stress [accessed 20 November 2014].
2. Acas. *Disciplinary and Grievance Procedures*. Norwich: TSO, 2009, www.acas.org.uk/dgcode2009 [accessed 13 November 2014].
3. Acas. Transfer of undertakings (TUPE). www.acas.org.uk/TUPE [accessed 13 November 2014].

8

Recent developments

GP federations
Employment tribunal changes
New health and work service in England and Wales

GP federations

NHS England has been developing Clinical Commissioning Groups (CCGs) for some time now. Partly as a result of this, coupled with a business efficiency drive, we have seen the development of federations of general practices.

In the context of general practice a federation is an organisation with collective arrangements covering two or more practices, with the aims of pursuing common objectives and maximising effective working.

For the purposes of this book we are concerned only with the employment of staff. General guidance on collaborative arrangements is offered without prejudice by the British Medical Association (BMA)[1] and by the Royal College of General Practitioners (RCGP).[2]

Staff employment

There are several ways of formulating the contractual terms of staff working in a GP federation or some other form of alliance. For all arrangements (see below) it is vital that matters be spelled out in writing.

First, a service-level agreement should be drawn up between the practices concerned to facilitate the proper management of the staff arrangements, including ensuring that appropriate service payments are made by the practices, and the establishment of a disputes procedure.

Next, the employment contracts of the staff concerned should be written to reflect the service-level agreement itself.

Shared staff

Where staff are shared by federated practices their contracts should state that the employer is either a list of all the practices, or it gives the name of the federation (if it has one). A job description should show the chain of command and who the individual's manager is. Terms of service must be clearly stated, bearing in mind there may be differences across the practices.

Correspondingly, the service-level agreement would show the financial responsibilities of each practice for shared staff. It should also cover who is responsible for managing the grievance and disciplinary procedures.

Seconded staff

In this situation an employee is 'hired out' to the other practices but is employed by only one of them and his or her contract states this. In such cases there should be a written agreement between the practices concerning how the employee's time might be charged for. Clearly, here, the practice doing the hiring out is the employer in law and has the concomitant responsibilities.

Finally, as the BMA points out, another arrangement is one whereby a practice employee may agree to work in another practice on a week-by-week 'loan' agreement. In this case the practice doing the 'loaning' is and remains the employer with all the attendant responsibilities.

Employment tribunal changes

In order to reduce the increasing number of tribunal applications new rules have come into force over the past two years. In 2014 it became a requirement that claimants wishing to lodge a tribunal application must first notify Acas to see if the dispute can be resolved. Acas then offers Early Conciliation to try to resolve the dispute quickly and cost-effectively.[3]

Previous government measures included the introduction in 2013 of fees for employees looking to take their employers to tribunal. Claimants wishing to bring a claim to the tribunal or appeal tribunal have to pay a fee beforehand. An initial fee is required to issue a claim and a further fee is payable if the claim proceeds to hearing.

There are two levels of fee, which will depend on the type of claim. This means, taking unfair dismissal as an example, that the cost of initiating a claim plus getting a hearing now amounts to £1200.

Last, for now, a penalty for breaches of employment law has been introduced. Such a penalty may be levied by an employment tribunal on an employer who loses a case.

The penalty will be 50% of the compensation payable to the employee, with a minimum of £100 and a maximum of £5000, where 'aggravating features' are present. These latter include: a large well-established employer with dedicated HR support; a long or repeated breach; and/or deliberate, malicious or negligent behaviour.

The introduction of tribunal fees for claimants has already had a big effect on the number of applicants.

Recent Ministry of Justice quarterly statistics for employment tribunals in 2014 reveal a 71% drop in claims compared with the same period in 2013.

Further, another significant statistic is that single claims were down one-third, possibly due in large part to the introduction of compulsory Acas Early Conciliation in May 2014.

New health and work service in England and Wales

According to government statistics, in each of the three years to October 2013, almost 1 million employees were on sick leave for a month or more on average. As part of the government's economic plan a new service will help employees and employers to manage sickness absence.

In future, employees on sick leave will be helped to return to work by providing them with occupational health support.[4]

Employees will normally be referred by their GPs, and key features of the service are that generic health and work advice will be offered through a website and telephone service (available to anyone) and Occupational Health assessments. The assessment service is designed to provide a free assessment of employees who have been, or who are likely to be, on sick leave for four weeks.

A resulting return to work plan will be shared with their employer and GP.

The service was launched in late 2014 with a phased roll-out and full introduction in 2015.

References

1. Collaborative GP alliances and federations. http://bma.org.uk/practical-support-at-work/gp-practices/collaborative-gp-alliances-and-federations [accessed 13 November 2014].
2. Imison C, Williams S, Smith J, Dingwall C. *Toolkit to Support the Development of Primary Care Federations*. London: RCGP, n.d. www.rcgp.org.uk/clinical-and-research/clinical-resources/~/media/19A1F84B41A04DFE8AAAF2F65FD3D757.ashx [accessed 13 November 2014].
3. Acas. Early Conciliation. www.acas.org.uk/index.aspx?articleid=4028 [accessed 13 November 2014].
4. Fit for Work. www.gov.uk/government/uploads/system/uploads/attachment_data/file/362480/fit-for-work.pdf [accessed 20 November 2014].

Appendix I

Useful sources of information

- Acas – excellent on detail of various procedures and practical advice (www.acas.org.uk).
- LRA – the Labour Relations Agency has responsibility for promoting the improvement of employment relations in Northern Ireland. A useful source of advice (www.lra.org.uk/).
- The Equality Commission for Northern Ireland – good on the specifics of Northern Ireland issues (www.equalityni.org).
- Gov.uk – very good on specific employment rights, it is much more user-friendly than it used to be (www.gov.uk/browse/employing-people).
- Equality and Human Rights Commission – has the mandate to challenge discrimination and to protect and promote human rights in Britain (www.equalityhumanrights.com/private-and-public-sector-guidance/employing-people/guidance-employers).
- Health and Safety Executive – good, clear website (www.hse.gov.uk/workers/employers.htm).
- CAB – the Citizens Advice Bureau provides people with the information they need to solve their own problems and to signpost them to appropriate advice when necessary:
    - *England*: www.adviceguide.org.uk/england/work_e/work_rights_at_work_e.htm
    - *Northern Ireland*: www.adviceguide.org.uk/nireland/work_ni/work_rights_at_work_e.htm
    - *Scotland*: www.adviceguide.org.uk/scotland/work_s/work_rights_at_work_s.htm
    - *Wales*: www.adviceguide.org.uk/wales/work_w/work_rights_at_work_e.htm.
- Agenda for Change terms of service – useful for reference (but don't try printing it off!) (www.nhsemployers.org/~/media/Employers/Documents/Pay%20and%20reward/AfC_tc_of_service_handbook_fb.pdf).

- BMA – the British Medical Association provides an Employer Advisory Service among many other things (http://bma.org.uk/practical-support-at-work/gp-practices/employer-advisory-service).
- RCGP – the Royal College of General Practitioners is the professional membership body for family doctors in the UK and overseas (www.rcgp.org.uk/).
- CIPD – the Chartered Institute of Personnel and Development is the professional body for HR and people development, with over 130,000 members internationally (www.cipd.co.uk).

Appendix II

Statutory payments

SMP, SPP, SAP
SSP
NI contributions
Qualifying earnings thresholds
Minimum wage

Table 1: Statutory Maternity, Paternity and Adoption Pay

Payment	To April 2015
Statutory Maternity Pay (SMP) weekly rate for first six weeks	90% of the employee's average weekly earnings
Statutory Maternity Pay (SMP) weekly rate for remaining weeks	£138.18 or 90% of the employee's average weekly earnings, whichever is lower
Ordinary Statutory Paternity Pay (OSPP) & Additional Statutory Paternity Pay (ASPP) weekly rate	£138.18 or 90% of the employee's average weekly earnings, whichever is lower
Statutory Adoption Pay (SAP) weekly rate	£138.18 or 90% of the employee's average weekly earnings, whichever is lower
SMP/OSPP/ASPP/SAP – proportion of payments recoverable from HMRC	92% if practice total Class 1 NICs (both employee and employer contributions) are above £45,000 for the previous tax year 103% if practice total Class 1 NICs for the previous tax year are £45,000 or lower

Statutory Sick Pay

The same weekly Statutory Sick Pay (SSP) rate applies to all employees. However, the amount an employer must actually pay an employee for each day he or she is off work due to illness (the daily rate) depends on the number of 'qualifying days' the employee works each week. See calculator below.

Remember – an employer is only responsible for paying SSP if:

- Class 1 National Insurance contributions are paid for the employee (or would do if not for the employee's age or level of earnings)
- you do not have an occupational sick pay scheme
- the employee was sick for four or more days in a row (including non-working days)
- the employee has told you he or she is sick within your own time limit (or seven days if you don't have one).

An online SSP calculator is available from Gov.uk.[1]

Table 2: **National Insurance contributions**

£ per week	2013 to 2014	2014 to 2015
Lower earnings limit, primary Class 1	£109	£111
Upper earnings limit, primary Class 1	£797	£805
Upper accrual point	£770	£770
Primary threshold	£149	£153
Secondary threshold	£148	£153
Employees' primary Class 1 rate between primary threshold and upper earnings limit	12%	12%
Employees' primary Class 1 rate above upper earnings limit	2%	2%
Class 1A rate on employer-provided benefits*	13.8%	13.8%
Employees' contracted-out rebate (for contracted-out salary-related schemes only)	1.4%	1.4%
Married women's reduced rate between primary threshold and upper earnings limit	5.85%	5.85%
Married women's rate above upper earnings limit	2%	2%
Employers' secondary Class 1 rate above secondary threshold	13.8%	13.8%
Employers' contracted-out rebate, salary-related schemes	3.4%	3.4%
Employers' contracted-out rebate, money-purchase schemes	N/A	N/A
Class 2 rate	£2.70	£2.75
Class 2 small earnings exception	£5725 per year	£5885 per year
Class 3 rate	£13.55	£13.90

Class 4 lower profits limit	£7755 per year	£7956 per year
Class 4 upper profits limit	£41,450 per year	£41,865 per year
Class 4 rate between lower profits limit and upper profits limit	9%	9%
Class 4 rate above upper profits limit	2%	2%
Additional primary Class 1 percentage rate on deferred employments	2%	2%
Additional Class 4 percentage rate where deferment has been granted	2%	2%

* Class 1A NICs are payable in July and are calculated on the value of taxable benefits provided in the previous tax year, using the secondary Class 1 percentage rate appropriate to that tax year.

From 1 October 2014, the following minimum wage levels apply (see Table 3).

Table 3: **National minimum wage**

Age	Hourly rate
21+	£6.50
18–21	£5.13
16–17	£3.79
Apprentice 1st year	£2.73

Reference

1. Calculate your employee's statutory sick pay. www.gov.uk/calculate-statutory-sick-pay/y [accessed 13 November 2014].

Appendix III

Written statement of employment particulars

An employer must give employees a 'written statement of employment particulars' if their employment contract lasts at least a month or more. This is not an employment contract as such but it will include the main conditions of employment.

The employer must provide the written statement within two months of the start of employment.

What a written statement must include

- The practice's name.
- The employee's name, job title or a description of work and start date.
- If a previous job counts towards a period of continuous employment, the date the period started.
- How much and how often an employee will get paid.
- Hours of work (and if employees will have to work Sundays, nights or overtime).
- Holiday entitlement (and if that includes public holidays).
- Where an employee will be working and whether he or she might have to relocate.
- If an employee works in different places, where these will be and what the employer's address is.
- How long a temporary job is expected to last.
- The end date of a fixed-term contract.
- Notice periods.
- Collective agreements.
- Pensions.
- Who to go to with a grievance.

- How to complain about how a grievance is handled.
- How to complain about a disciplinary or dismissal decision.

What a written statement does not need to include

(But it must say where the information can be found.)

- Sick pay and procedures.
- Disciplinary and dismissal procedures.
- Grievance procedures.

Appendix IV

Guidance on disciplinary procedures

The Acas Code of Practice 2009

This statutory code provides basic practical guidance on discipline (and grievance) handling in the workplace. It came into effect on 6 April 2009. Unlike the 2004 code, it does *not* require employers and employees to follow mandatory steps in the process.

Employment tribunals will use the code when considering relevant cases, taking into account factors such as the size and resources of a business. If a tribunal regards a failure by either the employee or the employer to follow the code as unreasonable, it will have the power to adjust awards up or down by up to 25%.

What follows is a synopsis of the code, focusing on disciplinary procedures. The full code and guidance can be accessed online.[1]

Keys to handling disciplinary issues in the workplace

1. Establish the facts of each case

An investigation of potential disciplinary matters should be carried out promptly to establish the facts of the case. This may require an investigatory meeting with the employee before proceeding to any disciplinary hearing. Otherwise, the investigatory stage will be the collation of evidence by the employer for use at any disciplinary hearing.

In misconduct cases, *where practicable*, different people should carry out the investigation and disciplinary hearing.

An investigatory meeting should not by itself result in any disciplinary action. Although there is no statutory right for an employee to be accompanied at a formal investigatory meeting, such a right may be allowed under an employer's own procedure.

In cases where suspension with pay is considered necessary, this should be as brief as possible, should be kept under review and it should be made clear that this suspension is not considered a disciplinary action.

2. Inform the employee of the problem

If there is a disciplinary case to answer, the employee should be notified of this *in writing*. This notification should contain sufficient information about the alleged misconduct or poor performance and its possible consequences to enable the employee to prepare to answer the case at a disciplinary meeting. Copies of any written evidence, which may include witness statements, should be included with the notification.

The notification should also give details of the time and venue for the disciplinary meeting and advise the employee of his or her right to be accompanied at the meeting.

If an employee is charged with, or convicted of, a criminal offence this is not normally in itself reason for disciplinary action. Consideration needs to be given to what effect the charge or conviction has on the employee's suitability to do the job and the employee's relationship with his or her employer, work colleagues and patients.

3. Hold a meeting with the employee to discuss the problem

The meeting should be held without unreasonable delay while allowing the employee reasonable time to prepare his or her case.

Employers and employees (and their representative) should make every effort to attend the meeting. At the meeting the employer should explain the complaint against the employee and go through the evidence that has been gathered. The employee should be allowed to set out his or her case and answer any allegations that have been made. The employee should also be given a reasonable opportunity to ask questions, present evidence and call relevant witnesses. They should also be given an opportunity to raise points about any information provided by witnesses. Where an employer or employee intends to call relevant witnesses they should give advance notice that they intend to do this.

Where an employee is persistently unable or unwilling to attend a disciplinary meeting without good cause the employer should make a decision on the evidence available.

4. Allow the employee to be accompanied at the meeting

Employees have a statutory right to be accompanied by a representative where the disciplinary meeting could result in:

- a formal warning being issued; or
- the taking of some other disciplinary action; or
- the confirmation of a warning or some other disciplinary action (i.e. appeal hearings).

The chosen representative may be a fellow employee, a trade union representative or an official employed by a trade union. A trade union representative who is not an employed official must have been certified by his or her union as being competent to accompany an employee.

The representative should be allowed to address the hearing to put and sum up the employee's case, respond on behalf of the employee to any views expressed at the meeting and confer with the employee during the hearing. The representative does not, however, have the right to answer questions on the employee's behalf, address the hearing if the employee does not wish it or prevent the employer from explaining his or her case.

5. Decide on appropriate action

After the meeting the employee should be informed in writing of the outcome. Where misconduct is confirmed or the employee is found to be performing unsatisfactorily it is usual to give the employee a written warning. A further act of misconduct or failure to improve performance within a set period would normally result in a final written warning.

If an employee's first misconduct or unsatisfactory performance is sufficiently serious, it may be appropriate to move directly to a final written warning. This might occur where the employee's actions have had, or are liable to have, a serious or harmful impact on the organisation.

A first or final written warning should set out the nature of the misconduct or poor performance and the change in behaviour or improvement in performance required (with a timescale). The employee should be told how long the warning will remain current. The employee should be informed of the consequences of further misconduct, or failure to improve performance, within the set period following a final warning. For instance, it may result in dismissal or some other contractual penalty such as demotion or loss of seniority.

A decision to dismiss should only be taken by a partner who has the authority to do so. The employee should be informed as soon as possible of the reasons for the dismissal, the date on which the employment contract will end, the appropriate period of notice and his or her right of appeal.

Some acts, termed gross misconduct, are so serious in themselves or have such serious consequences that they may call for dismissal without notice for a first offence. But a fair disciplinary process should always be followed, before dismissing for gross misconduct.

Disciplinary rules should give examples of acts that the employer regards as acts of gross misconduct. These may vary according to the nature of the organisation and what it does, but might include things such as theft or fraud, physical violence, gross negligence or serious insubordination.

6. Provide employees with an opportunity to appeal

Where an employee objects to the disciplinary action taken against him or her, the employee should be allowed to appeal against the decision. Appeals should be heard without unreasonable delay and ideally at an agreed time and place. Employees should let employers know the grounds for their appeal in advance *in writing*.

- The appeal should be dealt with impartially and, *wherever possible*, by a manager who has not previously been involved in the case.
- Employees have a statutory right to be accompanied at appeal hearings.
- Employees should be informed in writing of the results of the appeal hearing as soon as possible.

7. Overlapping grievance and disciplinary cases

Where an employee raises a grievance during a disciplinary process the disciplinary process may be temporarily suspended in order to deal with the grievance. Where the grievance and disciplinary cases are related it may be appropriate to deal with both issues concurrently.

Reference
1. Acas. *Disciplinary and Grievance Procedures*. Norwich: TSO, 2009. www.acas.org.uk/dgcode2009 [accessed 13 November 2014].

Appendix V

Employment tribunals

Composition
Procedures, settlements, etc.
Compensation awards

The employment tribunal system is largely independent of the ordinary courts. Tribunals have a narrowly defined jurisdiction covering most of the employment rights established by legislation. They were originally designed to provide a relatively cheap, informal and speedy means of adjudicating small-scale employment disputes.

The proceedings are meant to be informal, but this is generally not the case. Although wigs and gowns are not in evidence, they are formal affairs. For example, evidence is given on oath (or after affirmation), witnesses are cross-examined and legal submissions are presented. Generally, the pattern of proceedings follows orthodox court procedure.

A tribunal is composed, as the name suggests, of three individuals. There is a presiding employment judge (generally a solicitor or barrister who can sit alone for some hearings) and two lay members drawn from a panel after consultation with employer and employee organisations. The deliberate combination of legal expertise and working environment common sense is intended to make each tribunal suited to employment disputes.

The great majority of claims heard by tribunals are unfair dismissal complaints or redundancy payment claims or both together. They do however have jurisdiction over a large number of statutory provisions relating to employment matters. Apart from unfair dismissal, tribunals also cover breaches of the Equality Act, breaches of contract and many, many others. Claims (and responses) must now be presented online using prescribed forms.

Either party in a tribunal may apply for *further particulars* of the other party's case. These are designed to reveal what the case *is*, while *discovery* may be sought to reveal the *evidence* that might prove the case. All relevant documents should be submitted in a bundle prior to the hearing. Required documentation generally includes the following:

- letter of appointment or contract of employment
- disciplinary rules and procedures

- any written warnings, notes of verbal warnings
- notes of meetings
- letter of dismissal
- witness statements.

Before the full hearing, a *case management hearing* may be held. Here the tribunal will consider whether either party's case has any reasonable prospect of success. The case may not be dismissed, but the tribunal can issue a warning to the party pursuing a weak case that it does so at risk as to costs and witness expenses at the full hearing. Nowadays these are rare. Also a timetable will be set for the progress of the case.

At the full hearing the proceedings are similar to a magistrates' or sheriff court hearing and are open to the public and press. Beforehand, each party, together with their representatives and witnesses, will wait in separate rooms until called into the tribunal. Witnesses will only enter when called and may only leave after their evidence with the permission of the tribunal. The party who has the burden of proof usually opens (and will generally make the final submission). In an unfair dismissal case it is the respondent who has to prove the fairness of the dismissal, and therefore who opens the proceedings.

On opening, the documents submitted in the bundle will be taken as read and the first witness will be called immediately. In unfair dismissal cases, the respondent (employer) must prove that the *reason* for the dismissal was fair, and that the dismissal was a *reasonable* response to the employee's action.

The normal rules as to questioning – examination, cross-examination and re-examination – of witnesses apply, i.e. no leading questions, except in the main witness's evidence. Any witness statements from individuals not present must be agreed in advance with the other party. The respondent's case is then closed.

The claimant's case will then be heard in similar fashion including witnesses if appropriate. Both may then make a final submission to the tribunal, with the respondent finishing in unfair dismissal cases. At this stage the key facts of the case will be summarised, and any weaknesses in the other side's case pointed out. Also, any relevant case law will be referred to. The tribunal may then retire to consider their decision. Rarely, a verdict will be given verbally on the day, but generally a full written judgment with reasons is given later.

On costs, a tribunal has the power to make an award against the loser, should they consider the party to have been unreasonable. During the hearing for unfair dismissal, the parties may submit a reasoned estimate of the *award* that is being sought. The award made consists of two separate elements, the basic award and the compensatory award.

The *basic award* is calculated according to the applicant's age and length of service, and is subject to reduction for contributory fault. The *compensatory award* is the amount of purely *financial loss* and expenses 'in consequence of the dismissal'. The total is subject to a ceiling of one year's (net) pay for unfair dismissal but is *unlimited* for discrimination cases. A further reduction may be applied for a failure to mitigate loss.

Prior to the hearing, Acas will be involved in an attempt to settle the case by means of agreeing a conciliation settlement – generally a cash sum to be paid to the claimant by the respondent. This avoids a public hearing and is particularly useful where it is feared that weaknesses in the case may result in losing, or if bad publicity is feared. It should always be considered. Negotiations would generally be conducted through the parties' representatives and are now a formal requirement before the case is allowed to proceed to a hearing.

The Employment Tribunals Service has published statistics on the level of compensation made for the 12 months to 31 March 2014, as set out on Table 1.

Table 1: Employment tribunal statistics

Claim	Average	Median	Maximum
Unfair dismissal	£11,813	£5016	£3,402,245*
Race discrimination	£11,203	£5513	£162,593
Sex discrimination	£14,336	£8039	£168,957
Disability discrimination	£14,502	£7518	£236,922
Religious discrimination	£8131	£3191	£22,762
Sexual orientation discrimination	£8701	£6824	£27,659
Age discrimination	£18,801	£6000	£137,000

*Although the maximum awarded by a tribunal for unfair dismissal exceeds the statutory cap (currently £76,574), it should be noted that the cap does not apply where the reason for dismissal is for whistleblowing or raising certain health and safety issues.

For an overview of the law relating to unfair dismissal see Chapter 5.

Appendix VI

The Equality Act 2010

Protected characteristics
Forms of discrimination
Harassment and victimisation
Disability
Remedies

This long-awaited act followed more than four years of reviews, discussions and consultations. It applies to 'Great Britain', namely England, Wales and Scotland. The act does not apply to Northern Ireland. Here there is protection against discrimination on grounds of race, sex, age, religious belief and/or political opinion, sexual orientation, or because of disabilities. See the NIdirect website for further information.[1]

The majority of the act came into force in October 2010 and, to quote the Equality and Human Rights Commission (EHRC), it:[2]

[b]rings together over 116 separate pieces of legislation into one single Act. Combined, they make up a new Act that provides a legal framework to protect the rights of individuals and advance equality of opportunity for all.

Discrimination means treating someone *unfairly* because of *who they are*. The Equality Act protects against discrimination *by employers* as well as most service providers and public bodies. Under the act it is against the law to discriminate against someone because of a personal characteristic, e.g. disability or age.

Protected characteristics

In order to harmonise the various discrimination strands that had developed under previous legislation the act collectively terms them as 'protected characteristics'.

The nine protected characteristics under the act are:

- age
- disability
- gender reassignment
- marriage and civil partnership

- pregnancy and maternity
- race
- religion or belief
- sex
- sexual orientation.

See below for definitions.

Forms of discrimination

The act defines the various kinds of discrimination with reference to the protected characteristics. These types of discrimination largely replicate those found in previous legislation but there are some important changes that materially alter the scope of protection.

Direct discrimination

Direct discrimination occurs when someone is treated less favourably than another person because he or she:

- *has* a protected characteristic
- is *thought* to have a protected characteristic
- *associates* with someone who has a protected characteristic.

This definition of direct discrimination applies to all protected characteristics. In relation to the protected characteristic of age *only*, direct discrimination can be justified if it is a proportionate means of achieving a legitimate aim. Separate provisions exist in respect of discrimination against a woman on the grounds of pregnancy or maternity – no male comparator is required.

Association and perception

The definition of direct discrimination also covers a situation where someone is treated less favourably than another person because he or she is thought to have a protected characteristic (discrimination by perception) or because he or she associates with someone who has a protected characteristic (discrimination by association).

Indirect discrimination

Indirect discrimination occurs when a policy or practice that applies to everyone *particularly* disadvantages people who share a protected characteristic.

Indirect discrimination can only be justified if you can show that the policy or practice is a proportionate means of achieving a legitimate aim.

Indirect discrimination had already applied to age, race, religion or belief, sex, sexual orientation, and marriage and civil partnership. It has now been extended to cover disability and gender re-assignment. It does not apply to pregnancy or maternity.

Harassment

Harassment is defined in the act as:
> unwanted conduct related to a relevant protected characteristic, which has the purpose or effect of violating an individual's dignity or creating an intimidating, hostile, degrading, humiliating or offensive environment for that individual.

Harassment applies to all protected characteristics except for pregnancy and maternity, and marriage and civil partnership.

The act specifically prohibits three types of harassment:

- harassment related to a 'relevant protected characteristic'
- sexual harassment
- less favourable treatment of a service user because he or she submits to or rejects sexual harassment related to sex or gender reassignment.

Liability for harassment by third parties who are not your employees (e.g. patients or contractors) was originally in the act but was repealed in October 2014.

Victimisation

Victimisation occurs when an employer subjects a person to a detriment because the person has carried out (or were believed to have or may carry out) what is referred to as a 'protected act'.

A protected act is any of the following:

- bringing proceedings under the act
- giving evidence or information in proceedings brought under the act
- doing anything that is related to the provisions of the act
- making an allegation that another person has done something in breach of the act.

The term 'detriment' has not been defined under the act but it can be inferred that if an action has the effect of *putting a person at a disadvantage*, or if it makes his or her position worse, such treatment will amount to a detriment.

The victim need not have a protected characteristic in order to be protected from victimisation under the act. For example, he or she could have been supporting a person with a protected characteristic who is making a claim. Claims for victimisation can only be brought by individuals and not groups.

Amendments have been made to the definitions of individual characteristics and these are discussed below.

Discrimination arising from disability

This was a new provision. Under the act a person discriminates against a disabled person if he or she treats the person unfavourably because of something *arising in consequence* of his or her disability, and this treatment cannot be justified as a proportionate means of achieving a legitimate aim. Unlike direct and indirect discrimination, this form of discrimination does not require the use of a comparator to establish less favourable treatment.

As an employer if you did not know and could not reasonably have been expected to know of the disabled person's disability, then the unfavourable treatment will not amount to discrimination. You must do all you can reasonably be expected to do to find out if an employee has a disability.

What is *explicitly* banned under the act however is to ask prospective employees about their health *before* offering them work, i.e. using health questionnaires to screen applicants. An employer must limit questions to the job itself, i.e. is the applicant able to carry out specific tasks in the job description?

Duty to make adjustments

The act consolidates and extends existing duties upon employers and suppliers of goods and services from the Disability Discrimination Act 1995 to make reasonable adjustments for disabled persons.

The duty is three-fold:
1. Where a *provision, criterion or practice* puts a disabled person at a substantial disadvantage in relation to a relevant matter in comparison with persons who are not disabled, the person to whom the duty applies must take reasonable steps to avoid the disadvantage
2. Where a *physical feature* puts a disabled person at a substantial disadvantage in comparison with persons who are not disabled, the person to whom the duty applies must take reasonable steps to avoid the disadvantage
3. Where a disabled person would, but for the provision *of an auxiliary aid*, be at a substantial disadvantage in comparison with persons who are

not disabled, the person to whom the duty applies must take reasonable steps to provide the auxiliary aid.

In relation to requirements where the provision, criterion or practice in question or the auxiliary aid required relates to the provision of information, 'reasonable steps' include making sure that the information is in an accessible format.

The duty referring to the provision of auxiliary aids only previously applied to premises and goods and services, but has now been extended to employment.

Remedies for unlawful discrimination

Claimants need *no qualifying service* and the employer can be ordered by an employment tribunal to pay compensation, including interest. This *does not have any limit* stated by the law and so can be quite large. It can include damages for the hurt feelings of the applicant and the loss of the chance of the job. This last part can go beyond the loss of the actual wages. The damages can also be increased if the employer's behaviour was insulting or malicious.

Thought to be the highest compensation in a UK discrimination case, a hospital consultant was awarded £4.5m in December 2011 for being hounded out of her job after becoming pregnant. A Leeds tribunal found that the doctor suffered race and sex discrimination at Pontefract General Infirmary, part of Mid Yorkshire Hospitals NHS Trust.

A tribunal can also recommend that the employer take action to correct the situation or limit the damage done to the applicant. However, the tribunal cannot force the employer to promote the employee or take on the applicant for the job. The tribunal can also make recommendations that an organisation take steps to eliminate or reduce the effect of discrimination on other employees (although this does not apply to equal pay cases).

The EHRC can also become involved if the case is a test case or it would be unreasonable for the applicant to act alone, e.g. an applicant up against a large company with much greater resources.

Definitions of protected characteristics

Age

The act protects people of all ages from unlawful discrimination. It is important to note that this is the only protected characteristic where direct discrimination may be justified, but employers may only be able to justify differential treatment on the grounds of age if they can demonstrate that the different treatment is a proportionate means of achieving a legitimate aim.

With regard to the *provision of goods and services* the protected characteristic of age came into force in 2012 and only protects those aged 18 or above.

Disability

The definition of disability is essentially the same as that in the Disability Discrimination Act 1995. A person has a disability if he or she:

- has a physical or mental impairment

and

- the impairment has a substantial and long-term adverse effect on his or her ability to carry out normal day-to-day activities.

The government has published guidance on the definition of disability at Gov. uk.[3]

Gender reassignment

The definition of 'transsexual' was altered for the purposes of the act. The act defines a transsexual person as someone who is proposing to undergo, is undergoing or has undergone a process (or part of a process) for the purpose of reassigning a person's sex.

Marriage and civil partnership

Discrimination on grounds of marriage or civil partnership is prohibited under the act.

Pregnancy and maternity

Discrimination of women on the grounds of pregnancy or maternity during pregnancy and any maternity period is prohibited under the act. There are different provisions covering the work and non-work context.

Race

The position on race remains unchanged under the act. It is unlawful to discriminate on grounds of colour, nationality or ethnic or national origins.

Religion and belief

Religion has the meaning usually given to it but belief includes religious and philosophical beliefs including lack of belief (e.g. atheism). To be included in the definition, a belief should generally affect life choices or the way the person lives.

Sex

Men and women are protected under the act and there has been no change to the substantive law.

Sexual orientation

Heterosexual, bisexual, gay and lesbian people remain protected under the act. There has been no change to the substantive law.

References
1. NIdirect. Introduction to discrimination. www.nidirect.gov.uk/index/information-and-services/employment/discrimination-at-work/introduction-to-discrimination.htm [accessed 13 November 2014].
2. Equality and Human Rights Commission. What is the Equality Act? www.equalityhumanrights.com/legal-and-policy/key-legislatures/equality-act-2010/what-is-the-equality-act [accessed 13 November 2014].
3. Definition of disability under the Equality Act 2010. www.gov.uk/definition-of-disability-under-equality-act-2010 [accessed 13 November 2014].

Appendix VII

Absence records template

1. Individual record

Table 1: **Attendance record, year commencing 1 January 2015**							
Name		*Absence by type, number of days and reason*					
Date of absence		*Self-certified*		*Certified*		*Other*	
Start	Finish	No. of Days	Reason	No. of Days	Reason	No. of Days	Reason

Table 2: **Annual total**	
Total days lost (all absence)	
No. of times absent	
Average length	

How to use

Keep the records on a spreadsheet. It is possible then to keep a running total of the absence of all practice staff throughout the year. This can be transferred automatically to the practice record.

Using the spreadsheet formulas it is then an easy matter to calculate practice totals, and the average for each category of absence for the practice as a whole.

2. Practice record

Table 3: **Attendance record – practice, year commencing 1 January 2015**

Name	Absence in days for year				Average length of absence for year			
	Self-certified	Certified	Other	Total	Self-certified	Certified	Other	All
Practice average								

Appendix VIII

Self-appraisal form

This is a form to help an employee prepare for appraisal.

Name: ....
Section: ....
Date of appraisal: ....

Your next appraisal meeting will take place on:
Date: ....
Time: ....
Place: ....

Purpose of the appraisal meeting:
To enable you to discuss, with your manager, your job performance and your future. The discussion should aim at a clearer understanding of:

1. The main scope and purpose of your job
2. Agreements on your objectives and tasks
3. Standards or targets for measuring your performance
4. Your training and future development.

You can prepare for the meeting and discussion by completing this form.

You may show this form to your manager. This will give him or her time to consider your problems and suggestions. If you do so, it will not be copied or filed without your permission.

If you prefer, you can use this form for your own guidance only, and not show it to anyone.

You will be given the opportunity to read the appraisal form prepared by your manager; you will be able to add your comments, and sign the appraisal form.

Bring the following to the appraisal meeting:

- your current job description
- your current action plan.

Self-appraisal

Name: ....

1. In the boxes below indicate the appropriate answers, and comment below.

		Yes	No
(a)	Do you have an up-to-date job description?		
(b)	Do you have an up-to-date action plan?		
(c)	Do you understand all the requirements of your job?		
(d)	Do you have enough time to discuss your work and action plans?		
(e)	Have you carried out the improvements agreed with your manager that were made at the last appropriate meeting?		

2. What have you accomplished, over and above the minimum requirements of your job description, in the period under review (consider the early part of the period as well as more recent events)?

   Have you made any innovations?
   ....
   ....

3. List any difficulties you have in carrying out your work. Were there any obstacles outside your own control that prevented you from performing effectively?
   ....
   ....

4. What parts of your job, do you feel you:
   (a) Do best? ....
   (b) Do less well? ....
   (c) Have difficulty with? ....
   (d) Fail to enjoy? ....

5. Have you any skills, aptitudes or knowledge not fully utilised in your job? If so, what are they and how could they be used?
   ....
   ....

6. Can you suggest training that would help to improve your performance or development?
   ....
   ....

7. Additional remarks, notes, questions or suggestions.
   ....
   ....
   ....
   ....

Appendix IX

Workplace discussions

Employees should have the opportunity to discuss their future plans and expectations in the short, medium and long term, through workplace discussions. A workplace discussion can either be initiated by the employee or by the practice manager at any time. The discussion is an opportunity for the practice and employees to plan jointly for the future.

Workplace discussions are extremely valuable. Having open and honest discussions with staff can help managers plan more effectively for the future and, where appropriate, can help facilitate the transition through a work career for both the individual and the department.

Whatever the age of an employee, discussing their future aims and aspirations can help an employer to identify their training or development needs and provide an opportunity to discuss their future work requirements.

For all employees these discussions may involve the question of where they see themselves in the next few years and how they view their contribution to the practice. A useful exercise is to ask open questions regarding an employee's aims and plans for the short, medium and long term. Some employers may find it useful to hold these discussions as part of their formal appraisal process.

The outcome of any workplace discussions should be recorded and held for as long as there is a business need for doing so. It would be good practice to give a copy to the employee.

Acas believes that training managers in how to conduct all types of workplace discussions is important if they are to be conducted fairly and effectively. There is further guidance in an Acas advisory booklet on *Age and the Workplace*.[1]

Summary

Avoid questions that may indicate discriminatory assumptions.

- Use open questions. What are the employee's aims:
  - in the short term?
  - In the medium term?
  - in the longer term?
- Record all discussions – copy employee.

- From Acas advisory agenda:
  - performance to date against targets, activities and outcomes
  - developmental or training needs
  - future plans (employer)
  - aims and aspirations (employee)
  - future performance.

Workplace discussions can be part of existing appraisal systems a practice may have or any other means of talking to employees. You do not have to call them by this name but by one that makes operational sense in your practice.

Reference
1. Acas. *Age and the Workplace: putting the Equality Act 2010 and the removal of the default retirement age (DRA) 2011 into practice.* London: Acas, 2014, Annex 2. www.acas.org.uk/media/pdf/e/4/Age-and-the-workplace-guide.pdf [accessed 20 November 2014].

Appendix X

Employment scenarios – with comments

Chapter 2 – The contract of employment

1. The practice has been invited to bid for the provision of a surgery at a local supermarket. Staff contracts show the location and hours that are worked at present.

   Could employees be made to staff the supermarket surgery?

Key issue

Whether or not you can 'make' them is the wrong approach.

Points to consider

- Do your homework: a) What is the legal position? b) Decide steps to take.
- This is a contract change – so agreement is required.
- Consult – call for volunteers?
- Set up package? What's in it for them?
- If necessary consider trial period, or perhaps a rotation?
- When agreed put it in writing.

2. It transpires that your most recently appointed receptionist has, by an oversight, not been issued with a written contract. She now wants to change her shifts and says that, anyway, nothing has been agreed about the hours she works.

   What is the position?

Key issue

A contract term does not need to be in writing to be binding.

Points to consider

- What did the receptionist accept when she accepted the job?
- Is there a letter of appointment stipulating the hours? Or an advertisement?
- If the receptionist has worked the shift hours for a week or so she would be deemed to have agreed to them. If she had only worked for a day or so nothing is fixed yet.
- An employment tribunal could be asked by the receptionist to make a declaration of contract terms – it would make a finding using the foregoing points.
- Discussing matters with the receptionist is highly advisable!

Chapter 3 – Managing disciplinary procedures

1. A patient has complained that a receptionist told her that her daughter was pregnant. She had been unaware of the fact.

   How do you deal with this?

Key point
There is a need to be open-minded when investigating possible scenarios.

Points to consider

- Did the receptionist speak to the mother?
- How did the receptionist learn of the daughter's pregnancy?
- This is potentially gross misconduct if the receptionist learned about it from the records – so hold a disciplinary meeting, with the receptionist allowed (encouraged?) to have a representative present.
- If gross misconduct it could be appropriate to dismiss.
- But if the receptionist learned from the daughter this is may be different. It may have been indiscreet but is it a breach of confidentiality?
- *Where* the receptionist learned of the pregnancy may also be relevant, e.g. was the receptionist told outside the surgery premises? Perhaps in a social setting?
- Judgements will vary on this but in the latter scenario it may be sufficient to give a written warning about referring to this sort of information.

2. A young receptionist appears for work with a stud through her nose.

   Can you do anything about this?

Key issue

The receptionist is doing a job that may require rules about appearance because patients are involved.

Points to consider

- Is there a practice rule about appearance in 'public'? Is such a rule necessary in the practice?
- Although not explicit, an implied requirement may relate to appearance.
- The rule (written or unwritten) must be discussed with the receptionist and the management expectations spelt out.
- A review should be set up after, say, one month to determine that the receptionist is complying.
- Failure to comply should result in a written warning followed by another review.
- If at the review, or earlier, the nose stud is still in evidence a final written warning may be given, followed if necessary by dismissal.

Chapter 4 – Performance management

1. A patient has complained in writing about the attitude of one of the receptionists, and colleagues have commented informally about her. She was spoken to about this around a year ago.

   What should you do now?

Key issue

Is this conduct or capability?

Points to consider

- Behaviour yes, but could training be required?
- Conduct – use disciplinary procedures, warnings, set up diaried reviews.
- Capability – appraise, establish cause, support? warn employee, review.

- Allow time for improvements.
- Regular reviews are essential.

2. One of your clerical staff is having problems coping with the records system. At her appraisal she says that she has never got used to computers and prefers the old days when everything was done by hand.

   How would you deal with this?

Key issue
It is reasonable to ask an individual to adapt to new (!) working methods.

Points to consider
- Support should be provided for training or re-training.
- Goals should be set for applying new skills – specific tasks undertaken.
- Regular appraisal, say, at three-monthly intervals (not annual) should be set up.
- If no improvement is forthcoming the individual must be warned her job is at risk.
- The practice disciplinary procedure must be used.
- The aim is improved performance but in the long term dismissal may be an outcome.

Chapter 5 – Terminating the contract

1. The senior partner tells you that one of the receptionists has sworn at him in the course of an argument and he 'wants her out'.

   How do you respond?

Key issue
If dismissal, is the reason fair? Maybe, but what about the procedure?!

Points to consider
- To satisfy a tribunal the Acas Code should be followed.
- Establish the facts of the case: who swore at whom?

- Inform the employee there is a problem with her behaviour (possibly a breach of the duty to act in good faith and fidelity).
- Hold a meeting with the employee to discuss the issue and allow the employee to be accompanied.
- Only then decide on appropriate action, which should be 'within the range of reasonable responses'.
- Provide employee with an opportunity to appeal.
- If necessary counsel the senior partner.

Incidentally, employers are not expected to have to tolerate an employee swearing at a manager or a colleague, even if it is an isolated occurrence. However, employers might take a more lenient approach if an employee uses bad language that is not directed at a particular person.

Clearly, an uncharacteristic outburst by a normally well-behaved employee might have other factors behind it, e.g. stress brought on by overwork or bullying of that person.

2. A fortnight before a receptionist is due to go on holiday she asks if she can bring it forward so that she can fly with friends. Because of staff shortages you have to refuse. The receptionist then goes sick for the week before her holidays.

   How do you deal with this?

Key issue
Would it be gross misconduct for the employee to feign sickness?

Points to consider
- Establish the facts.
- Speak to the employee on her return.
- It would be reasonable in the circumstances to seek some corroboration from the employee about the flight she took (and maybe from the airline?).
- If the employee had taken the earlier flight this would probably be at least misconduct.
- Any subsequent attempt, e.g. to forge a boarding pass, would almost certainly be gross misconduct.

- Despite the foregoing a reasonable procedure must be followed – the practice's own disciplinary procedures in this case.

Chapter 6 – Specific legal issues

1. Full-time staff are entitled to have bank holidays off. A part-time member of staff who does not work on Mondays wants time off in lieu for bank holiday Monday.

    What is the legal position?

Key issue

Part-timers should get the same holidays pro rata as full-timers.

Points to consider

- Time off in lieu for any specific public holiday is irrelevant.
- Whether or not the temp works on Monday is irrelevant.
- Full-timers get 5.6 weeks minimum paid holiday annually.
- Stay with the annual figure and calculate the annual total for any given part-timer. 'Full-time' hours are the hours your own 'full-timers' work – 35, 37.5 or 40 hours generally. The holiday total can be in days or hours.
- Back to the Monday bank holiday: the part-timer cannot get a day off for a Monday bank holiday since she does not work on Mondays. So long as her annual total of days/hours is in the correct proportion to full-timers she is being treated no differently from them.

A nice chore for practice managers is to work out each year in advance which days a part-timer is going to be off when the practice is closed and she would be otherwise working. The part-timer, like full-timers, has to take a day off when the practice is closed and this is subtracted from the annual holiday total. This should eradicate complaints of 'I never get a Monday holiday off' from some part-timers.

2. Your practice nurse mentions that her young daughter's child minder is (not for the first time) going to be unavailable, this time next Monday. The nurse would be working that day so she asks for the day off.

    How do you respond to this?

Key issue

An employee has a right to 'reasonable time off to deal with an emergency involving a dependant'.

Points to consider

- There is no requirement to pay an employee for time off to look after dependants; this will depend on the employment contract.
- An inference here may be that the practice nurse is abusing these leave provisions – 'not for the first time'.
- My dictionary defines an emergency as a 'sudden crisis requiring action'.
- Can something happening next week really be considered an emergency? If not, then dependant's leave is not appropriate.
- You could suggest the nurse takes a day's holiday, or she could apply for parental leave, but 21 days' notice would be required here.

This is an issue that might usefully be discussed at appraisal time, although this could be raised at any time. The nurse may wish to talk about reducing her hours.

Index

A

absence records 29–30
    templates 113–14
Acas 89
    Code on disciplinary procedures 39–40, 80, 97–100
    conciliation service 86, 103
Additional Paternity Leave 53, 55
adoption
    Statutory Adoption Pay 91
    see also maternity rights; parental leave; paternity rights
age discrimination 109–10
agency staff 4–5
annual leave entitlement 56–7
annualised hours 60
    see also flexible working
antenatal care, leave entitlement 49, 52
appeals
    against dismissal 41
    against flexible working decisions 62
appraisal techniques 74
appraisals 27, 71–5
    self-appraisal form 115–16
attendance records templates 113–14

B

behaviour
    misconduct 27
    performance management 21–4
    signs of stress 77
breach of contract 10–11
    constructive dismissal 42–3
bullying 32–4
business transfers, TUPE regulations 82–3

C

capability 26–7
case management hearings 102
cautionary tale, employment status 5–6
changing the contract 9–10
Citizens Advice Bureau (CAB) 89
compensation
    for unfair dismissal 40
    for unlawful discrimination 109
compensation awards, employment tribunals 103
compressed hours 60
    see also flexible working
conduct 27
    see also disciplinary procedures
constructive dismissal 33, 42–3
contract termination 11, 12, 37
    dismissal 38–43
    employment scenarios 122–4
    notice periods and pay 37–8
    redundancy 43–5
    unfair dismissal 38

contracts 2–3
    breach of 10–11
    changes to 9–10
    employment scenarios 119–20
    fixed-term (FTCs) 64–7
    legalities 7
    terms of 7–9

D

Data Protection Act 73
dependants' leave 57, 124–5
direct discrimination 106
disability, definition of 110
disabled employees 24–6
    discrimination against 108
    duty to make adjustments 108–9
disciplinary procedures 14–15, 40–1
    Acas Code of Practice 97–100
    appeals 16
    employment scenarios 120–1
    formal disciplinary meetings 16–19
    indications for 27
    overlap with grievance procedures 82
discrimination 3, 23, 73
    disabled employees 24–6
    Equality Act 2010 105–11
    forms of 106–8
    in job adverts 4
dismissal of employees 10, 15
    appeals 41
    constructive 42–3
    employment scenarios 122–4
    expiry of fixed-term contracts 65–7
    practical handling of 40–1
    reasonableness 39–40
    redundancy 43–5
    TUPE regulations 83–4
    unfair 38, 40
duties and responsibilities
    of employees 8, 79
    of employers 8–9, 67–8, 79

E

Employee Liability Information, TUPE regulations 83
employment scenarios
    contract termination 122–4
    contracts 119–20
    disciplinary procedures 120–1
    leave entitlement 124–5
    performance management 121–2
employment status 47–8
    assessment of 6
    a cautionary tale 5–6
    and fixed-term contracts 64–5
employment tribunals 101–3
    flexible working decisions 62
    recent changes 86–7
equality legislation 4, 55–6, 73
    Equality Act 2010 105–11
    information sources 89

F

family-friendly issues *see* dependants' leave; maternity rights; parental leave; paternity rights
federations 85–6
fixed-term contracts (FTCs) 64–7
flexible working 59–60
    appeals 62
    statutory application 60–2
flexitime 60

G

gender reassignment 110
GP federations 85–6
grievance procedures 80–2

H

harassment 34–5, 107
    disabled employees 25
health and safety 67–8
health and work service 87
home working 59
    see also flexible working

I

implied terms, contracts 7–9
indirect discrimination 106–7
information sources 89–90

J

job adverts 4
job sharing 59
    see also flexible working

K

'keeping-in-touch days' 50

L

Labour Relations Agency 89
leave
    for dependants 57, 124–5
    maternity 48–51
    parental 49–50, 52, 58–9
    part-timers 124
    paternity 51–5
    statutory entitlement 56–7
legalities 1–2
    contracts 7
    equality legislation 55–6, 105–11
    fixed-term contracts 64–7
    flexible working 59–62
    health and safety 67–8

    maternity rights 48–51
    parental leave 58–9
    part-time employees 63–4
    paternity rights 51–5
    statutory leave entitlement 56–7
    statutory rights 47
    Transfer of Undertakings (TUPE) regulations 82–4

M

Maternity Allowance 50
maternity rights 48–51
    equality legislation 110
misconduct 27

N

National Insurance contributions 92–3
national minimum wage levels 93
notice periods
    and fixed-term contracts 65–6
    termination of employment 37–8

O

Occupational Health 87
Ordinary Paternity Leave 52, 54
Ordinary Paternity Pay 91
overtime pay, part-time employees 63

P

parental leave 58–9
    see also maternity rights; paternity rights
part-time employees 59
    rights 63–4, 124
    see also flexible working
paternity rights 51–5
pay
    and dependants' leave 57

maternity rights 49–50, 91
national minimum wage levels 93
during notice periods 37
part-time employees 63
paternity rights 52, 54–5, 91
redundancy payments 45
Statutory Sick Pay (SSP) 91–3
pensions, contributions during maternity or parental leave 50
performance management
behaviour 21–4
bullying 32–4
capability 26–7
disability 24–6
disciplinary procedures 14–19, 97–100
employment scenarios 121–2
harassment 34–5
misconduct 27
sickness absence 27–32
unsatisfactory assessments 73
phased retirement 60
see also flexible working
poor performance 22, 24
capabilities 26–7
pregnancy
equality legislation 110
maternity rights 48–51
see also parental leave; paternity rights
protected acts, Equality Act 2010 107
protected characteristics, Equality Act 2010 105–6, 109–11
public holidays, leave entitlement 57, 124

R

racial discrimination 110
reasonableness of dismissal 39–40
redundancy 43–5
expiry of fixed-term contracts 65–7
during maternity or parental leave 51
TUPE regulations 83–4
redundancy payments 45
religious discrimination 110
resignation, constructive dismissal 42–3
responsibilities
of employees 8, 79
of employers 8–9, 67–8, 79
retirement, phased 60
rights 3–4
of agency staff 4–5
equality legislation 55–6, 105–11
fixed-term contracts 64–7
flexible working 59–62
maternity 48–51
parental leave 58–9
part-time employees 63–4
paternity 51–5
statutory 47
statutory leave entitlement 56–7
rules 13–14

S

seconded staff, GP federations 86
self-appraisal form 115–16
service provision transfers, TUPE regulations 83
sex discrimination 111
sexual orientation, equality legislation 111
Shared Parental Leave 49, 50, 52
shared staff, GP federations 86
sickness absence 27–32
attendance records templates 113–14
health and work service 87
Statutory Sick Pay (SSP) 91–3
skills 26
staff transfers, TUPE regulations 82–4
staggered hours 60
see also flexible working
Statutory Adoption Pay 91
statutory leave entitlement 56–7
Statutory Maternity Pay 49–50, 91

Statutory Paternity Pay 52, 91
Statutory Sick Pay (SSP) 91–3
stress 75–7
    behavioural and physical signs of 77
stress management programmes 78
stress policies 78–9
Sure Start Maternity Grant 50
suspension 97

##

temporary contracts 64–7
termination of contract *see* contract termination
terms of contracts 7–9
Transfer of Undertakings (TUPE) regulations 82–4

U

unfair dismissal 38
    compensation 40, 103
    and fixed-term contracts 65–6
    TUPE regulations 83–4
    see also employment tribunals

V

victimisation 107–8

##

workplace discussions 22–4, 117–18
written statements of employment particulars 2–3, 95–6

Lightning Source UK Ltd.
Milton Keynes UK
UKOW04f0309300916

284097UK00001B/9/P